महाभारतम्

MAHABHARATA

MIRIAM FERNANDES
& RAVI JAIN

ANCILLARY MATERIALS COMPILED & EDITED BY
KAREN FRICKER & LAWRENCE SWITZKY

COACH HOUSE BOOKS, TORONTO

Play copyright © Miriam Fernandes and Ravi Jain, 2023
Additional materials © their authors, 2023

first edition

Published with the generous assistance of the Canada Council for the Arts and the Ontario Arts Council. Coach House Books also acknowledges the support of the Government of Canada through the Canada Book Fund and the Government of Ontario through the Ontario Book Publishing Tax Credit.

LIBRARY AND ARCHIVES CANADA CATALOGUING IN PUBLICATION

Title: Mahabharata / by Miriam Fernandes and Ravi Jain.
Names: Fernandes, Miriam, author. | Jain, Ravi, author.
Description: A play.
Identifiers: Canadiana (print) 20230470807 | Canadiana (ebook) 20230470815 | ISBN 9781552454756 (softcover) | ISBN 9781770567900 (EPUB) | ISBN 9781770567917 (PDF)
Subjects: LCGFT: Drama.
Classification: LCC PS8611.E7486 M34 2023 | DDC C812/.6—dc23

Mahabharata is available as an ebook: ISBN 978 1 77056 790 0 (EPUB), 978 1 77056 791 7 (PDF)

Purchase of the print version of this book entitles you to a free digital copy. To claim your ebook of this title, please email sales@chbooks.com with proof of purchase. (Coach House Books reserves the right to terminate the free digital download offer at any time.)

TABLE OF CONTENTS

PLAYWRIGHTS' NOTE

By Miriam Fernandes and Ravi Jain

Mahabharata was once described to us as a dense forest of stories that one needs to carve one's own path through. That act of carving, ploughing, and weeding feels true to the journey we've been on these past eight years. Which trees to start from? Which branches to trim so that others can enjoy the light? Do we take the most direct path through, or the winding scenic route?

At times, adapting this epic has felt equivalent to wrestling the wind. In one moment the story is unbelievably powerful and clear in its intentions. In the next moment its intentions slip through your fingers, impossible to grasp. It is vast and complex, constantly surprising you and contradicting itself. And for thousands of years it has been told over and over, in many different ways. How could we tell *Mahabharata* today and have its messages resonate with modern audiences?

Our team felt that exploring how this story has been told over the centuries was just as important as the story's plot. Our telling blends traditional and modern, East and West, and includes various forms of Indian dance, storytelling, live music, and even a Sanskrit opera. We've also tried to mimic many people's real-life experience: receiving these stories through an interpretation and lesson over a meal (in *Khana and Kahani*). Each of these forms of storytelling help to unlock *Mahabharata*'s meanings – they help us reach beyond words and narrative to access its spiritual and philosophical underpinnings.

It's rare to experience *Mahabharata* from beginning to end in one sitting. (Here we've made it into two two-hour sittings, plus the meal.) It needs time. It requires perspective. Its stories stay with you – their contradictions become the subject of conversations and debates, and as we age those meanings change.

After eight years of sitting with this epic, the revelation of the *Mahabharata* for us has been to learn not to become distracted by the forest, or concerned with the wind, but to immerse oneself even deeper into the earth, travelling into the labyrinth of its roots. As the Storyteller cautions, 'Don't be confused by plots. Within this forest of stories flows a river of wisdom. That is your true inheritance.'

PLACES IN *MAHABHARATA*
10TH CENTURY BCE

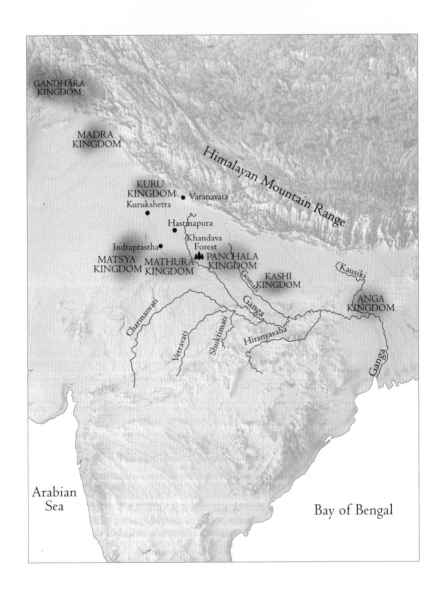

Map by Daniele De Vecchi

MAHABHARATA FAMILY TREE

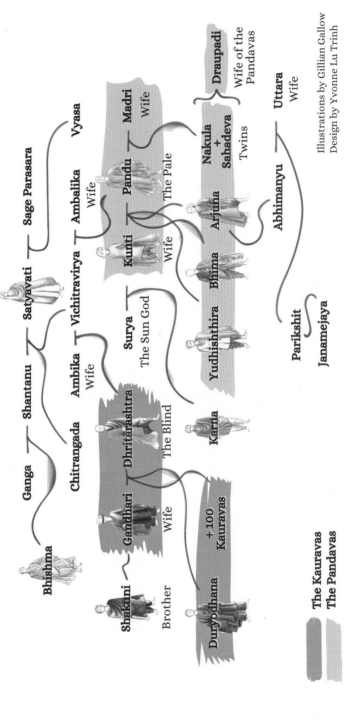

Illustrations by Gillian Gallow
Design by Yvonne Lu Trinh

The Kauravas
The Pandavas

DRAMATIS PERSONAE

In order of appearance.

Storyteller: The sutradhara, or weaver of the threads.

King Janamejaya: Son of King Parikshit (who has just died). Performing a ritual sacrifice of snakes to avenge his father's death.

Takshaka: A snake who was orphaned in the fire of Khandava Forest. Killer of King Parikshit to avenge his family.

Shantanu: King of Hastinapura, husband of Satyavati.

Satyavati: Fisherwoman who marries King Shantanu.

Fisherman: Adoptive father of Satyavati.

Bhishma: King Shantanu's son from a previous marriage. The heir apparent to the throne of Hastinapura.

Gods: Voices of the devas that ring down from heaven.

King of Kashi: Father of Amba, Ambika, and Ambalika.

Amba: Eldest of the three princesses of Kashi.

Shiva: God of Destruction. Part of the trinity of gods who rule the universe, along with Brahma the Creator and Vishnu the Preserver.

Ensemble 1: Narrator for act 1, scene 5, 'Daughter of a Fish.'

Vyasa: Son of Satyavati and a sage. Father of Dhritarashtra and Pandu. Original author of the *Mahabharata*.

Ambika: Second princess of Kashi, sister to Amba and Ambalika, mother of Dhritarashtra the Blind.

Ensemble 2: A narrator in act 1, scene 6, 'Birth of Dhritarashtra and Pandu.'

Dhritarashtra the Blind: Son of Vyasa and Ambika, also known as the Blind King.

Ambalika: Third princess of Kashi, sister to Amba and Ambika, mother of Pandu the Pale.

Pandu the Pale: Son of Vyasa and Ambalika, also known as the Pale King.

Gandhari: Princess of Gandhara who marries Dhritarashtra the Blind, eventually becoming Queen of Hastinapura. Mother of Duryodhana and ninety-nine Kaurava sons. Sister of Shakuni.

Shakuni: Brother of Gandhari.

Kunti: Princess of the kingdom of Mathura. Wife of Pandu the Pale. Mother of the Five Pandavas. Biological mother of Karna, who she gave up at birth.

Madri: Princess of the kingdom of Madra. Second wife of Pandu the Pale. Mother to Nakula and Sahadeva.

Deer 1 and 2: Sages who have disguised themselves as deer to make love in the forest.

Surya: The Sun God. Father of Karna.

Karna: Son of Surya and Kunti, but was abandoned as a baby. Raised by a chariot driver and is seen as someone of lower class.

Yudhishthira: Son of Kunti and Dharma, the God of Death and Lord of Righteousness. The most honest man.

Bhima: Son of Kunti and Vayu, God of the Wind. Has incredible strength.

Arjuna: Son of Kunti and Indra, God of the Heavens, Thunder, Lightning, Storms, and War. Known for his skills as an archer and warrior.

Nakula and Sahadeva: Sons of Madri and the Ashwini Twins. Nakula is the most beautiful man, and Sahadeva is the wisest.

Duryodhana: Son of Gandhari and Dhritarashtra. Born from a ball of flesh, which was divided up and placed in jars of ghee to incubate. Eldest of the Kaurava princes.

Shakuni's Father: Father to Gandhari and Shakuni. Killed by Bhishma through starvation.

Drona: Teacher to the Kauravas and Pandavas in the art of war.

Drupada: King of Panchala, childhood friend of Drona.

Ekalavya: A youth who lives in the forest. A highly skilled and disciplined archer.

Parashurama: A revered weapons master. Teacher of Drona and Karna.

Draupadi: Daughter of King Drupada. Born of fire, she is Lord Shiva's answer to Drupada's prayer to have a child who will divide the Kuru Clan.

Krishna: An incarnation of Lord Vishnu (one of the supreme deities along with Brahma and Shiva) on earth. Nephew of Kunti, and first cousin of the Pandavas.

Sharada: Performer in *Khana and Kahani*.

Miriam: Storyteller for *Part 1: Karma* and *Part 2: Dharma*, and performer in *Khana and Kahani*.

Sanjaya: Aid to King Dhritarashtra. Granted the gift of divine sight by Krishna to see everything happening on the battlefield during the war and narrate it to King Dhritarashtra.

Voice of Krishna in the *Bhagavad Gita* Opera: A divine manifestation of Krishna during the *Bhagavad Gita*. We hear God's voice as an operatic aria.

Abhimanyu: Young son of Arjuna.

Indra: God of the Heavens.

Dharma: God of Death (also known as Yama) and Lord of Righteousness.

A note on casting: This production relies on an ensemble of performers, including a live band in *Part 1: Karma*. In act 1 especially, the actors sometimes work as an ensemble, playing many parts, supporting the band musically, and sometimes sharing the role of narration with the Storyteller. Ensemble 1 and 2 are specific examples of the ensemble sharing narrative text. At times the musicians and singers also speak text (such as when they take on the voices of the gods in act 1, scene 3, 'Bhishma's Vow').

A NOTE ON STAGING

The first production featured an intergenerational cast of actors from the South Asian diaspora. They were a community of storytellers who played all the roles, changing as each character was called into action. Once an actor became their principal character(s), they no longer switched into other characters – the exception being double casting. Some casting defied gender and age.

The form evolved throughout the production, starting with traditional storytelling by a fire, then moving to 'poor theatre' with no props and actors miming objects. The actors' bodies were engaged through dance and physical performance to make the story come to life. Over the course of the play, more theatrical elements were added: chandeliers floated down from the sky, a large throne sat on a lush carpet, an ominous disc descended from above. These elements moved us into a more contemporary theatre world. In *Part 2: Dharma*, some elements of the technology jumped forward thousands of years (live cameras, projections, eighteen large-screen TVs), while other elements (costumes, dirt, fire) remained in the ancient world. Live music was a major element in *Part 1: Karma*, and pre-recorded underscoring and microphones in *Part 2: Dharma* created a more intimate, cinematic feel.

All of these are ways to engage with the myriad forms that we as humans have used to tell stories, particularly a story as ancient as *Mahabharata*, which has been told over and over in so many different ways. Each of those ways is as important as the content; the 'how' is the mechanism through which we receive the poetic and deep spiritual meanings hidden within the stories.

Throughout the duration of the show, travelling through all of these forms and ways to tell a story, one feels transported, like we went on a long journey to a place that seemed foreign and yet so familiar.

A note on dialogue:
' / ' is an overlap.
' … ' is a trailing off.
' – ' is an interruption.
'Storyteller as Character' is the Storyteller performing that character's text.
'Character/Storyteller' is the character and Storyteller's lines overlapping.

ORIGINAL CAST AND CREATIVE TEAM

Mahabharata
Written and adapted by Ravi Jain and Miriam Fernandes,
using poetry from Carole Satyamurti's *Mahabharata: A Modern Retelling*
Original concept developed with Jenny Koons
A Why Not Theatre Production
In association with Barbican, London
Commissioned and presented by the Shaw Festival

ﷺ

Mahabharata was originally presented at the Shaw Festival in Niagara-on-the-Lake, Canada, in February–March 2023. *Mahabharata* had its international premiere at the Barbican Centre, London, in October 2023.

Mahabharata includes, with permission, some text from Carole Satyamurti's *Mahabharata: A Modern Retelling*, published by W. W. Norton & Company, Devdutt Pattanaik's *Jaya: An Illustrated Retelling of the Mahabharata*, published by Penguin Random House India, and the poetry of Rabindranath Tagore.

ﷺ

Cast, Shaw Festival
Yudhishthira / Shantanu: Shawn Ahmed
Krishna / Shakuni's Father / Parashurama: Neil D'Souza
Shiva / Amba / Drupada / Pandu: Jay Emmanuel
Storyteller: Miriam Fernandes
Dhritarashtra / Fisherman: Harmage Singh Kalirai
Duryodhana: Darren Kuppan
Arjuna / Ensemble 1: Anaka Maharaj-Sandhu
Gandhari / Draupadi / Ensemble 2: Goldy Notay
Kunti / Drona: Ellora Patnaik
Voice of Krishna in the *Bhagavad Gita* Opera: Meher Pavri
Shakuni / Sanjaya: Sakuntala Ramanee
Karna / Satyavati: Navtej Sandhu
Bhima: Munish Sharma
Bhishma: Sukania Venugopal

Understudies: Varun Guru, Karthik Kadam, Anand Rajaram, Ronica Sajnani, Ishan Sandhu

Band
Conductor / Guitar: John Gzowski
Band Leader / Voice: Suba Sankaran
Bass / Keyboard / Music Contributions: Dylan Bell
Percussion / Music Contributions: Gurtej Singh Hunjan
Tabla / Music Contributions: Zaheer-Abbas Janmohamed
Bansuri / Voice / Music Contributions: Hasheel Lodhia

Creative Team
Director: Ravi Jain
Associate Director: Miriam Fernandes
Set Designer: Lorenzo Savoini
Costume Designer: Gillian Gallow
Lighting Designer: Kevin Lamotte
Associate Lighting Designer: Mikael Kangas
Projections Designer: Hana S. Kim
Associate Projections Designer: Ann Slote
Original music and sound design: John Gzowski and Suba Sankaran
Traditional Music Consultant: Hasheel Lodhia
Choreographer: Brandy Leary
Khana and Kahani Storyteller and Artistic Associate: Sharada K Eswar
Production Manager: Crystal Lee
Lead Producer: Kevin Matthew Wong
Producer: Michelle Yagi
Why Not Theatre Executive Director: Karen Tisch

Production Stage Manager: Allan Teichman
Stage Manager: Neha Ross
Assistant Stage Managers: Ashley Ireland, Tamara Protić

Assistant Set and Costume Designer: Rose Tavormina
Costume Consultation: Sarena Parmar, Jay Emmanuel, Brandy Leary, Sharada K Eswar
Assistant Projections Designer: Cameron Fraser
Assistant Sound Designer: Olivia Wheeler

Video Engineers: Daniel Carr, Matthew Mellinger
Technical Director, Video: Daniel Bennett

Opera Translation / Text Adaptation: Sharada K Eswar
Opera Guest Recording Artist (mrdangam): Trichy Sankaran

Kathakali Contributions: Jay Emmanuel
Odissi Contributions: Ellora Patnaik
Dance Captain: Jay Emmanuel

Fight Director: John Stead
Fight Captain: Munish Sharma

Assistant Producer / Company Manager: Matt Eger
Associate Producer, Why Not Theatre: Fatima Adam
Associate Production Manager: Maya Royer
Assistant Production Manager: Jacob Danson-Faraday

Why Not Theatre, May 2023
Co-Artistic Director and Founder: Ravi Jain
Co-Artistic Director: Miriam Fernandes
Executive Director: Karen Tisch

Special Projects Manager: Mary Anderson
ThisGen Fellowship Producer: Intisar Awisse
Grantwriter: Erin Brandenburg
Administrative and Development Coordinator: Karishma Bristy
Senior Development Advisor: Jessica Kamphorst
Production and Technical Manager: Crystal Lee
Marketing and Communications Manager: Yvonne Lu Trinh
Operations and Development Manager: Katy Mountain
Finance Director: Sarah Newkirk
Senior Producer and Artistic Associate: Kevin Matthew Wong
Senior Producer: Michelle Yagi

Contributing Why Not Team: Kelly Read, Owais Lightwala, Kendra Bator,
    Kira Allen

Bhishma awes the crowd with his skill in combat at the swayamvara of the three princesses of Kashi. From act 1, scene 4.

The secret birth of Karna is told in the form of an Odissi dance. From act 1, scene 10, with Pandu (Jay Emmanuel) and Kunti (Ellora Patnaik).

Drona trains the Kauravas and Pandavas in the art of war. From act 2, scene 17.

Dhritarashtra welcomes the Pandavas at court and divides the kingdom in half, hoping to make peace between the families. From act 4, scene 29, with Dhritarashtra (Harmage Singh Kalirai) and the cast of Mahabharata.

Shakuni proposes that Duryodhana challenge Yudhishthira to a game of dice in order to win back the Pandavas' half of the kingdom. From act 4, scene 33, with Duryodhana (Darren Kuppan), Dhritarashtra (Harmage Singh Kalirai), Shakuni (Sakuntala Ramanee), and Gandhari (Goldy Notay).

As the Kauravas attempt to strip Draupadi in the gambling hall, Krishna performs a miracle to make her robes endless. From act 4, scene 35, with Draupadi (Goldy Notay).

The Pandavas send Krishna as their envoy to the Kauravas to negotiate for peace. From act 6, scene 2, with Karna (Navtej Sandhu), Duryodhana (Darren Kuppan), Krishna (Neil D'Souza), Drona (Ellora Patnaik), and Dhritarashtra (Harmage Singh Kalirai).

Krishna reveals his divine manifestation to Arjuna through the Bhagavad Gita, interpreted here as an opera. From act 7, scene 13, with Krishna (Neil D'Souza), the Voice of Krishna (Meher Pavri), and Arjuna (Anaka Maharaj-Sandhu).

Kunti appeals to Gandhari to stop Duryodhana from starting a war with the Pandavas. From act 6, scene 9, with Kunti (Ellora Patnaik) and Gandhari (Goldy Notay).

The Storyteller narrates as Arjuna and Krishna ride out into the middle of the battlefield before the war begins. From act 7, scene 13, with the Storyteller (Miriam Fernandes), Arjuna (Anaka Maharaj-Sandhu), and Krishna (Neil D'Souza).

As Bhishma is struck down during battle, Lord Shiva recounts the liberation of Amba's soul through Kathakali. From act 8, scene 15, with Lord Shiva (Jay Emmanuel).

Kunti approaches Karna on the battlefield to beg him to abandon the Kauravas and join her sons. From act 8, scene 18, with Karna (Navtej Sandhu) and Kunti (Ellora Patnaik).

Bhima and Duryodhana's mace fight concludes the war. From act 8, scene 20, with Duryodhana (Darren Kuppan) and Bhima (Munish Sharma).

In the wake of the war, Yudhishthira visits Bhishma on his bed of arrows seeking guidance on the future. From act 9, scene 23, with Arjuna (Anaka Maharaj-Sandhu), Bhima (Munish Sharma), Yudhishthira (Shawn Ahmed), and Bhishma (Sukania Venugopal).

PART 1
KARMA
THE LIFE WE INHERIT

ACT I: INHERITANCE

SCENE I: THE KHANDAVA FOREST

As the audience enters, six musicians are seated at the back of a bare stage, improvising vocals and playing a mix of traditional South Asian and Western instruments. There is a large circle of red dirt on the stage and a number of wooden stools placed around the perimeter of the circle. The back wall of the theatre is exposed, and there is a bar lying close to the stage floor behind the musicians with thick ropes tied onto it. Performers come on and off the stage as the musicians play, doing pranam in respect for the space and musicians, and in preparation for the performance. With the house lights still on, the Storyteller walks onstage to the centre of the circle as the band plays the final tihai.

STORYTELLER: I take you to the Khandava Forest. A dense wilderness where no humans live, but it is inhabited by many plants, animals, and mystical creatures that live between the heavens and the earth. It was a cool, dry day when the young prince, Arjuna, was walking through the forest, leaves crunching under his feet as he walked. Arjuna and his brothers had recently inherited this land. It wasn't exactly the kind of place you'd imagine kings to live …

So Arjuna is walking, deep in thought, when he hears a rustle in the bushes, and when he looks, an old man emerges, frail and shivering. He puts out his hands toward Arjuna:

'My son, please give me something to eat, I am starving!'

'Of course!' says Arjuna. 'Let me go find you some food –'

'It's not food I want,' says the stranger.

Arjuna is confused. 'What can I bring you then?'

'I am Agni, I am fire itself. This Khandava Forest, this is the feast I crave.'

Arjuna is taken aback. He looks around at the trees, the birds, and then he looks back at Agni. He has made a promise that he will feed this god; he cannot take his word back now.

Arjuna is one of the greatest archers in the world. He takes an arrow out of his quiver and sets the tip alight, then, stringing his bow, he pulls back and lets the arrow fly.

It hits its target easily, a pile of dry grass which immediately goes up in flames, and Agni begins to eat.

He makes his way through the grass, which hasn't been rained on for weeks. Then he begins to climb the bushes, the trees, the vines – consuming, gobbling, hungry for more.

As the smoke and flames become thicker, the animals of the forest begin to panic. They try to escape, but everywhere they turn more flames pop up. By now the fire has spread everywhere, devouring the nests and dens of animals, blazing through underground tunnels, burning creatures alive. The air is full of the smell of smoke and death. The animals cry out to the gods, 'Save us!'

And Indra, God of the Heavens, hears their cry. He sends down buckets of rain to quench the flames, but Agni turns to Arjuna – 'Stop him!' – and Arjuna shoots a stream of magical arrows into the sky, creating a canopy between the heavens and the earth, so that not one drop of water penetrates the ground.

Agni eats, and eats, and eats for days until, finally, he is satiated. Everything is destroyed – nothing but smoke rises off the charred earth. There is only one survivor of the fire: a snake, named Takshaka, who is left orphaned. The fire consumed his home, his family, everything.

Takshaka watches through the smoke as the figure of Arjuna disappears into the distance, and he swears to himself that he will have revenge on Arjuna and his descendants for what has been done to his family.

SCENE 2: THE SNAKE SACRIFICE

STORYTELLER: One hundred years pass.

We travel to the kingdom of Hastinapura, where the king is hiding in a tower, because he has been cursed that in seven days' time, he will be killed by a snake. The king locks himself away from his family, his subjects, he is terrified, he can't eat, he can't sleep. On the seventh day, the starving king bites into an apple, and inside that apple is a worm. That worm transforms into the snake Takshaka, who sinks his fangs into the king's neck, and he dies instantly.

The king's son, Janamejaya, cries out, 'I will avenge my innocent father! Call the priests, light the sacrificial fire, I will have every snake in the land burned!'

People from all the lands gather, and a huge fire is lit in the centre of the kingdom of Hastinapura.

The storyteller lights a match and places it in a fire bowl. The upstage coiled ropes are slowly drawn up; they look like snakes suspended in the air. The ensemble enters and takes their places on wooden stools around the outside of the red circle of dirt.

The hymns of the priests drag snakes out of the ground, the trees, the sky, and into the pit of fire. Everyone watches, some furious, some terrified, but nobody says anything, until one brave young person speaks up.

'Stop this senseless killing! This is against dharma!'

Stillness.

The snakes hang suspended over the fire.

'Who dares speak to the king like that?'

'I do. King or not, I must speak.'

'Who are you? What clan do you belong to?'

'My name is Astika, and my uncle is the King of the Snakes.'

The crowd erupts: 'He's one of them! Burn him!'

'It's not so simple,' says Astika. 'My father was a human, my mother was a snake. I am you and your enemy. I take no sides, but if you don't listen to me, my king, you will deny peace to all your descendants.'

'Speak,' says Janamejaya.

'My King, one hundred years ago, your great-grandfather, Arjuna, set fire to the forest of Khandavaprastha. Takshaka lost his entire family in that fire. In taking your father's life, he has his revenge. Now you take your revenge by burning snakes in your sacrificial hall. More orphans will be created. More vengeance will be wreaked. Is that what you want, my king?'

'I do this for justice!' says Janamejaya.

'Takshaka killed your father for justice. Who decides what justice is?'

Janamejaya thinks about this. 'Did my ancestors, the Pandavas, not fight for justice when they defeated the Kauravas in the war of Kurukshetra?'

'No, my king, they fought for dharma.'

'Tell me more.'

Storyteller picks up the fire bowl from the centre of the circle and carries it to the downstage edge of the red circle of dirt, where she places it on the ground.

So Astika calls for a storyteller, and the entire kingdom settles in around the fire, snakes hanging in the air above them. Before beginning, the storyteller says, 'As you listen to this tale, do not be distracted by the plots. Within this forest of stories flows a river of wisdom. That is your true inheritance.'

SCENE 3: BHISHMA'S VOW

The music shifts. During this chapter, all the action happens inside the red circle. The actors sit on the perimeter of the circle on wooden stools when not in scenes. The Storyteller is a kind of conductor; as she speaks, characters emerge, and the world of the stories comes to life through the ensemble.

STORYTELLER: The storyteller begins with Janamejaya's great-great-great-grandfather, while he was still prince, waiting to inherit the throne. His father, King Shantanu, had fallen madly in love with a fragrant fisherwoman –

SHANTANU: Satyavati!

STORYTELLER: Every day Satyavati rowed her boat across the river, and every day the king watched her longingly.

SHANTANU: Marry me!

SATYAVATI: Okay!

FISHERMAN: Ah, ah, ah …

The Fisherman stops them before they touch.

STORYTELLER: The only obstacle was Satyavati's father, the Fisherman.

FISHERMAN: King Shantanu, I know how these things work. You have a son, and in the course of time, he will ascend the throne, and my poor daughter and her children will be cast adrift, cut off without one coin to call their own. I cannot allow my daughter to marry you.

BHISHMA: Sir, with all due respect, your daughter, a fisherwoman, is the love interest of my father, the king. And you want to impede this marriage?

FISHERMAN: Yes, we are fisherpeople, but our only chance at rising up is through this union here. You are the heir apparent, and your children will inherit the throne from you. My daughter's family will be disinherited.

BHISHMA: The solution is simple: I renounce the title of heir apparent. Satyavati's son shall be the next king of Hastinapura.

FISHERMAN: Strong-armed one, it's not that I don't trust you. I know you would never break a promise, but how do I know your sons will feel the same? They may feel entitled to take the throne back from my grandson.

BHISHMA: I would never let that happen. All my life, I vow to protect the king.

FISHERMAN: You would favour Satyavati's son over your own?

BHISHMA: Yes.

FISHERMAN: I don't believe you. I still withhold consent.

BHISHMA: Then, here and now, and in the name of all that I hold sacred, in the name of my guru, of my mother, and of dharma, I vow to live a life of celibacy. I shall never marry, I shall never father children.

STORYTELLER: The heavens open up, the gods shower flowers on his head.

GODS: From now on, you will be known as Bhishma, he who has taken the most terrible of vows. As a boon, we grant you the power to choose the exact moment of your death.

STORYTELLER: With Bhishma's vow, Satyavati marries the king, she becomes queen, and they are very happy. In that happiness, they have two sons, and before you know it, it's time for them to get married. So Satyavati tasks Bhishma with finding them brides. The custom for marriage at this time is for princes to enter a competition, a swayamvara, where they display their skill and the princesses select their husband. So Bhishma travels across the land to a swayamvara held for the three princesses of the kingdom of Kashi.

SCENE 4: THE THREE PRINCESSES

The music and ensemble explode in celebration; we are at the swayamvara.

KING OF KASHI: Welcome to you all, so happy to have you! Today my daughters Amba, Ambika, and Ambalika choose their husbands, what happiness!

STORYTELLER: Bhishma bursts through the door.

BHISHMA: There are several ways by which a Kshatriya may claim a bride, but the one that commands the greatest respect is to bear her off by force. This I shall do. Fight me if you dare … I am blessed by the gods, no one can kill me!

The ensemble takes on Bhishma in a cartoonish fight. At the end of the sequence, Bhishma is the only one standing.

STORYTELLER: Bhishma returns to Hastinapura with all three princesses.

The three princesses kneel at Satyavati's feet.

SATYAVATI: Amba, you are the eldest of the three princesses. You will be the queen and inherit this kingdom! What is wrong?

AMBA: Queen Satyavati, I am promised to Prince Shalva, he is my true love.

SATYAVATI: You may go back, child, and live happily here with your husband.

STORYTELLER: So Amba returns to Shalva. But he says,

SHALVA: You have been won by the prince. You belong to him now.

STORYTELLER: So Amba returns to Satyavati's son. But he also rejects her.

Amba returns to Bhishma.

AMBA: Bhishma, you have to marry me now.

BHISHMA: I cannot marry you, Amba. My vow forbids it.

AMBA: You have ruined my life. You have taken a vow. I will also take a vow: I vow to never eat and never sleep until I am the cause of your death.

BHISHMA: No one can kill me, Amba.

The following sequence is performed by Amba as a dance.

STORYTELLER: Amba leaves the kingdom that day with the spark of revenge lit in her heart. She swears revenge on Bhishma and travels to a peak in the Himalayas, where she lights a fire and prays to Lord Shiva, God of Destruction. Amba stands on one foot for twelve years in the snow and ice, until finally she hears the voice of Shiva.

SHIVA: Amba, you shall be the cause of Bhishma's death, but only in your next life.

STORYTELLER: Amba leaps into the fire.

Amba's dance takes her to the firebowl downstage, where she takes the ash of the fire and tosses it into the air at the climax of the dance/music.

With Amba gone, her two sisters marry Satyavati's sons. The family is complete. But before anyone can have babies, King Shantanu dies.

Satyavati cries out.

And then Satyavati's eldest son dies.

Satyavati cries out.

And then …

SATYAVATI: Ah, Bhishma! My youngest son, the prince, is dead!

STORYTELLER: Queen Satyavati has a problem.

SATYAVATI: There is no heir to the throne of Hastinapura. Bhishma, you have to do something!

BHISHMA: I've done all I can.

SATYAVATI: You must become king. You would rule wisely and justly for all of time –

BHISHMA: But I renounced the throne forever. I made a vow –

SATYAVATI: Surely the fate of our family is reason enough to break your vow!

Bhishma is silent.

SATYAVATI: If you will not be king, we need to produce grandchildren, rightful heirs to the throne. You must father children with Ambika and Ambalika.

BHISHMA: I can never father children!

SATYAVATI: We will lose all that we have: our land, our palaces ... All that we have built will be taken away from us.

BHISHMA: My vow is everything. Words, once spoken, can never be unspoken without dishonour. Sun may lose its brilliance, moon its lustre, rain may withhold its blessing from the earth, fire may grow cold and colour colourless before I will consent to break my word.

SATYAVATI: If you will not do what is necessary, then I know who will ...

She closes her eyes.

SCENE 5: DAUGHTER OF A FISH

STORYTELLER: To understand what happens next, I need to take you back to Satyavati's father ...

We travel back in time and see the Fisherman casting his net into the water.

ENSEMBLE 1: The Fisherman. He was out for his daily catch, when a large fish swam into his net.

The Fisherman mimes cutting open the fish.

Inside the fish he found a tiny baby girl. The fisherman raised her as his own child.

FISHERMAN/STORYTELLER: Satyavati!

ENSEMBLE 1: But having been born from the belly of a fish, and hanging out with fishermen all day, you can only imagine ... the smell. And she could not get rid of it! So even though she was beautiful, no one would come near her.

SATYAVATI: I wish my body had a heavenly fragrance.

ENSEMBLE 1: One day, a sage offered to make her fragrant in exchange for the chance to lie with her. So she agreed and he summoned a mist to envelop them. Her wish came true and she became so fragrant that nobody could resist her. And that very day she gave birth to a son who instantly became a man.

The Storyteller enters the scene as Vyasa.

SCENE 6: BIRTH OF DHRITARASHTRA AND PANDU

SATYAVATI: Vyasa. My son. I need your help. You must father children with my two widowed daughters. Give me a grandson who will grow to be the perfect king.

STORYTELLER AS VYASA: Mother, I will do this on one condition. I have spent decades in the forest, in deep meditation, sorting the holy scriptures. I'm unwashed. Give me one year to ready myself, then I will father the heirs to the throne.

SATYAVATI: No, we don't have time! A kingdom with no king cannot flourish; it must be done at once! Ambika!

Ambika appears.

In the dead of night your brother-in-law will come into your room. Welcome him, so you can bear a son to save the Bharatas.

ENSEMBLE 2: Ambika was expecting Bhishma to come to her, but instead she saw …

Ambika sees Vyasa. She covers her eyes. Blackout.

SATYAVATI: My wise son, will a perfect king be born?

STORYTELLER AS VYASA: He will. He will be immensely strong, courageous, learned, and wise; he will be the father of one hundred sons. But because his mother would not look at me, he will be born without sight. He will be called Dhritarashtra the Blind.

SATYAVATI: No! A blind man cannot be king! Ambalika?

Ambalika appears.

Child, in the dead of night your brother-in-law will come into your room. You must not close your eyes. Welcome him, so you can bear a son to save the Bharatas.

Ambalika sees Vyasa and turns pale. A blinding white light.

My wise son, will a perfect king be born?

STORYTELLER AS VYASA: A second baby will be born, but because his mother turned pale when she saw me, he will be born as white as the moon. He will be called Pandu the Pale.

SATYAVATI: I fear this baby is weak. A weak man cannot be king! Go again!

STORYTELLER: But this time the princesses are savvy. Secretly, they send their maid into the bedroom to take their place. And this maid is not afraid – she welcomes Vyasa as a lover.

The maid approaches Vyasa and reaches out her hand, and he takes it. Blackout.

And a third son is born! His name will be Vidur, and he will be the wisest man on earth. He will speak truth, he will be gentle and wise. But …

SATYAVATI: The son of a maid will never sit on the throne.

STORYTELLER: Queen Satyavati has heirs to the throne of Hastinapura: Dhritarashtra the Blind and Pandu the Pale.

SCENE 7: MARRIAGE

STORYTELLER: Twenty years pass!

We are at a wedding. Kunti and Pandu put garlands around each other's necks. They are a young couple happily in love.

Kunti, the princess of the kingdom of Mathura, has just chosen Pandu the Pale to be her husband. Pandu not only wins a beautiful bride, he acquires more land. The kingdom grows.

Madri moves toward Pandu and Kunti.

Pandu takes a second bride, Madri, princess of the kingdom of Madra. Even more land. The kingdom grows.

The wedding party leaves as the musical tone changes. Gandhari prepares for her wedding.

Gandhari is princess of the kingdom of Gandhara, and this is her brother, Shakuni.

GANDHARI: Brother, did you see him? What's he like? Describe him to me, tell me everything!

SHAKUNI: Sister, he is very tall.

GANDHARI: How tall?

SHAKUNI: Like a tree. He would be your shade from a brightly shining sun.

GANDHARI: Ohh! How wonderful, what else?

SHAKUNI: He is very strong.

GANDHARI: How strong?

SHAKUNI: He would move mountains to clear your path.

GANDHARI: Is he handsome?

SHAKUNI: Oh, sister, he is unmatched! The moon itself is jealous of his glow!

GANDHARI: Oh, I'm so relieved! But you seem to be full of doubt.

SHAKUNI: Sister, your husband-to-be is blind …

GANDHARI: Why does this make you sad?

SHAKUNI: Because he will never see your beauty, he will never set eyes upon your children …

Dhritarashtra slowly makes his way to Gandhari (as if in another time/space).

GANDHARI: And what about the worlds we will discover with our scent? And our taste, and our touch?

They touch.

DHRITARASHTRA: Your voice is soothing. Like music.

She puts his hands on her face, then she pulls away and tears a piece of cloth from her clothing.

What are you doing?

Gandhari wraps the cloth around her eyes as a blindfold.

GANDHARI: You will be the last person in this world that I see.

She brings his hands to her face again; he discovers the blindfold.

I want to experience the world in the way you do. From now on, we will always be equal. We will neither lead nor follow, but we will walk side by side through life.

SCENE 8: CHOOSING A KING

STORYTELLER: It's as if the marriages of the princes confer a blessing on the land. It is a time of abundance. Rains are plentiful, the soil is rich and nourished, the earth is happy. And now, it's time to choose a king.

DHRITARASHTRA: Bhishma, you have been like a father to me. Tell me: will I be king?

BHISHMA: I …

DHRITARASHTRA: Yes?

BHISHMA: I don't know.

DHRITARASHTRA: Am I the eldest son?

BHISHMA: Yes.

DHRITARASHTRA: The rightful heir?

BHISHMA: You are.

DHRITARASHTRA: Am I strong, kind, loyal to my family and kingdom?

Bhishma is silent.

Do you not believe I would be a great king?

We come back to Gandhari and Dhritarashtra.

GANDHARI: What's wrong?

DHRITARASHTRA: Gandhari, my brother Pandu has been crowned king. You will never be a queen.

GANDHARI: You are the rightful heir! How short-sighted they are to underestimate you.

DHRITARASHTRA: Let us make a baby, quickly, before Pandu makes one. /We will have a son to reclaim what is rightfully ours.

STORYTELLER: /We will have a son to reclaim what is rightfully ours.

SCENE 9: PANDU'S EXILE

Music and time pass.

STORYTELLER: Pandu the Pale is a good king, but his real passion is for hunting. One day while out on his daily hunt, he comes across two deer in the act of making love.

Two actors enter the space, using mudras to signify the deer. Pandu approaches them slowly and shoots an arrow through the two deer as they mate.

BOTH DEER: Ahhhhhh!

They hold on to each other as they struggle to breathe.

DEER 1: You are a king, you have all the wealth of the world, and yet you hunt for pleasure!

DEER 2: You have acted brutally and out of greed. You will share our fate.

DEER 1: The moment that you take one of your wives into your arms, you will die instantly.

Kunti rushes toward Pandu.

PANDU: Do not touch me! We can never have children. What kind of king can I be? Better to renounce the world, shave my head, wander the land homeless, without blessings, without possessions, eating what I beg. I renounce my royal robes and my worldly wealth. I leave the kingdom to my brother, Dhritarashtra the Blind.

Pandu, Kunti, and Madri leave the kingdom. Dhritarashtra is adorned as king with royal robes and jewellery.

STORYTELLER: Dhritarashtra the Blind and Gandhari are king and queen of Hastinapura. Glowing inside with pride, they make love, and …

GANDHARI: We will have an heir to the throne.

SCENE 10: KUNTI'S SECRET

STORYTELLER: Pandu, Kunti, and Madri go into exile, deep in the mountains, each carrying a darkness inside them. Their dreams of parenthood had vanished. That one arrow changed the course of their lives forever.

PANDU: Why do you follow me? I have nothing to offer you.

KUNTI: Pandu, I may have the solution to our problem …

PANDU: What do you mean?

KUNTI: When I was young, a brahmin taught me how to summon gods to do my bidding. If you agree, I'll call upon a god to give us a son.

PANDU: A god?

KUNTI: Yes.

PANDU: Have you used this mantra before?

KUNTI: Never.

PANDU: So how do you know it works?

KUNTI: I just know.

STORYTELLER: Kunti had a secret. Many years ago when she was just a girl, she was out in the sun and she decided to test out this mantra.

Flashback to Kunti as a child. The musicians chant an invocation to the sun god, 'Om Suryaya Namaha.'

And there he was, huge and luminous, the Sun God himself!

The actor playing Kunti performs this memory as an Odissi dance. The dialogue is voiced by the Storyteller.

STORYTELLER AS SURYA: Kunti, you summoned me, what can I do for you?

STORYTELLER AS KUNTI: My lord, I did not think you would appear! I was just playing. Please go back to the sky!

STORYTELLER AS SURYA: Kunti, you cannot call forth the sun simply to dismiss him. This mantra carries a special power. I am going to give you a child who will be unrivalled in prowess.

STORYTELLER AS KUNTI: Will this child have golden armour as you have?

STORYTELLER AS SURYA: He will. He will have a golden chest plate to protect him from harm and divine earrings to light up his face. He will be called Karna.

Kunti performs the dance of Karna's birth.

STORYTELLER: And Karna is born, as radiant as the sun. But Kunti is just a girl. She knows she cannot return home with a child. So she takes the baby and walks down to the river. She wraps the baby in a blanket and places him in a basket and she whispers …

STORYTELLER AS KUNTI: You are so lucky to have a father who will watch over you. How lucky is the woman who will nurture you, hear your first words, and guide your first steps!

STORYTELLER: The baby started to cry, so she picked him up to rock him to sleep.

A lullaby is being sung in the distance.

The disapproving sun set quickly that night.

Lullaby reprise.

Kunti kept singing, walking alongside the floating basket.

Lullaby reprise.

Until her baby, Karna, the son of the Sun, vanished into the horizon.

Lullaby reprise fades out of the flashback and we return to the previous scene.

SCENE II: BIRTH OF THE PANDAVAS

PANDU: Have you used this mantra before?

KUNTI: Never.

PANDU: So how do you know it works?

KUNTI: I just know. Which God shall I call?

PANDU: First, call on Dharma, King of Justice, God of Death, and Lord of Righteousness!

Throughout this sequence, Kunti performs a dance for the birth of each son.

STORYTELLER: Surrounded by a garland of flames, the god Dharma appears. Instantly, a son is born.

Yudhishthira appears.

He will be called Yudhishthira; he will be the most honest man in the world.

PANDU: This time call on Vayu, God of the Wind.

STORYTELLER: Incomparably beautiful and powerful beyond measure, Vayu rides in on a chariot driven by one thousand white horses. And Bhima is born.

Bhima appears.

Offspring of the god who stirs up cyclones and tornadoes, Bhima is the strongest man in the world.

PANDU: Call another! Kunti, this time you must choose a god.

STORYTELLER: So Kunti chooses Indra, God of the Heavens. And blazing before them, a lightning bolt in hand, Indra rides in on a white elephant. From the god of lightning, thunder, storms, and war, Arjuna is born to save her.

Arjuna appears.

Heavenly voices ring out, the Earth blooms for his birth: Arjuna was born to save her, to fight a great battle in her name!

PANDU: Call another!

STORYTELLER: Kunti sees in Madri the same longing to mother children, so she shares the mantra with Madri, who calls the Ashwini twins, and from them, twin boys are born: Nakula and Sahadeva. Together, these five boys, the sons of gods, possess all the qualities of a great king. Yudhishthira the Most Honest of Men, Bhima the Strong, Arjuna the Warrior, Nakula the Beautiful, and Sahadeva the Wise. These five boys will be called the Pandavas.

There is a musical flourish as the dance ends. Blackout.

SCENE 12: BIRTH OF THE KAURAVAS

Lights slowly rise on Gandhari, who is on the ground, arms around her belly.

STORYTELLER: Meanwhile, Gandhari has been pregnant for two years.

GANDHARI: Are you in there? Are you moving? Can you hear my voice? Give me a sign: a kick, a turn, anything to show me you're there.

STORYTELLER: The news of the births of the Pandavas reaches Gandhari. She turns to her servant.

GANDHARI: Take a rod and hit me.

Beat.

> HIT ME!
> HIT ME!
> HIT ME!

The percussion of the drums act as a call and response to Gandhari's cries of 'hit me,' until she gives birth.

Is it a boy?

STORYTELLER: No.

GANDHARI: Is it a girl?

STORYTELLER: No. It is a ball of flesh, as cold as iron.

GANDHARI: It was said that we would have a hundred children.

STORYTELLER: Gandhari and Dhritarashtra are instructed to divide the ball into one hundred pieces and place each piece into a jar of ghee. Gandhari waits every day until, finally, the first jar cracks.

Duryodhana is born with a blood-curdling cry.

GANDHARI: He sounds so beautiful. Oh, my son! Come to me. My prince!

Rattling, howling, thunder, jackals outside.

DHRITARASHTRA: Bhishma, what is that noise?

Horses braying.

BHISHMA: The earth is speaking.

DHRITARASHTRA: What is she saying?

BHISHMA: This baby will bring ruin and disaster to generations to come. For the sake of your great-great-grandchildren, kill this baby. Sacrifice the one to save us all.

DHRITARASHTRA: Sacrifice him? My newborn son? Bhishma, how can you ask this of me?

GANDHARI: My husband, my king, come and meet your son.

BHISHMA: My king, the clouds weep. The earth is afraid of this child.

GANDHARI: Let the rains thrash and the jackals cry! These are not signs or omens, Bhishma. Isn't it our duty to protect the weak? Isn't that dharma?

BHISHMA: Queen Gandhari –

GANDHARI: He is the prince. He is the heir apparent. You will bow to him in years to come. We will name him Duryodhana the Invincible.

STORYTELLER: One by one, the other jars begin to crack, giving birth to Duryodhana's ninety-nine brothers. These hundred boys will be called the Kauravas.

Through a short movement sequence, Duryodhana transforms from a baby into a toddler, a child, an adult, and begins to train to fight. The tension in the music and movement build to a flourish. Blackout.

SCENE 13: DEATH OF PANDU

STORYTELLER: Years pass. One night, there is a knock on the door. Kunti and the Pandavas come bearing terrible news.

KUNTI: Pandu and Madri were overcome by the desire to make love. The moment that they touched, the curse came true. They died instantly.

DHRITARASHTRA: Oh heavy news. My brother Pandu, jewel of this kingdom, gone? Bhishma, how can one day be full of such joy and such immense pain?

BHISHMA: Bodies are born, they flourish, age, and die. But the soul is never born and can never be killed.

KUNTI: King Dhritarashtra, Queen Gandhari, we have lost everything. I didn't know where else to go …

GANDHARI: Kunti, be at ease here. Leave the forest behind you and live here as my sister.

BHISHMA: You are home where you belong. Now let the Pandavas take their place beside their hundred Kaurava cousins.

Bhishma brings Kunti into the palace. Dhritarashtra and Gandhari are left alone.

GANDHARI: Dhritarashtra, my husband, you seem troubled.

DHRITARASHTRA: Gandhari, my mind tosses like the ocean. For these past years while the Pandavas have lived in the forest, I have reigned as king. What will the return of Pandu's sons mean for our family?

GANDHARI: We must rule according to Dharma: they have nothing and we must protect them as if they were our own children.

DHRITARASHTRA: Yes.

GANDHARI: And yet fear clings to you.

DHRITARASHTRA: Prince Yudhishthira is Pandu's eldest son. Prince
  Duryodhana is our eldest son.

GANDHARI: Who will inherit the kingdom?

The storyteller takes centre stage as Dhritarashtra and Gandhari exit.

ACT 2: DIVISION

SCENE 14: GROWING UP

STORYTELLER: The Pandavas were awed by Hastinapura. All they had ever known was living in the forest, so moving into the palace was like a rebirth: soft beds, exquisite food, servants on every hand ... And meeting their cousins was a joy.

Yudhishthira and Duryodhana play a game. Duryodhana wins the first round.

At first, the Kauravas and Pandavas played well together, but it wasn't long before they tried to outdo each other, to prove who was best.

Bhima and Duryodhana face off for round two. Duryodhana is more agile but Bhima is bigger and stronger. Bhima wins.

DURYODHANA: Redo, redo! This was distracting!

STORYTELLER: Bhima liked to tease and bully his Kaurava cousins, and Duryodhana, quick to anger, was an easy target.

Bhima and Duryodhana play again.

DURYODHANA: You cheated!

BHIMA: I won fair and square! What are you, blind?

ARJUNA: Like your dad!

DURYODHANA: Say that again!

Duryodhana lunges for Arjuna. Bhima holds him back easily. Duryodhana is no match for Bhima's strength.

SCENE 15: BHIMA AND THE NAGAS
AND SHAKUNI'S BACKSTORY

Bhima freezes at the centre of the circle. Duryodhana circles him.

STORYTELLER: Month by month, year by bitter year, in Duryodhana corrosive hatred grew.

DURYODHANA: Uncle!

Shakuni enters, limping.

STORYTELLER: Shakuni is Gandhari's younger brother and Duryodhana's favourite uncle.

DURYODHANA: I want to make Bhima pay!

SHAKUNI: Then fight him.

DURYODHANA: I can't, Bhima is too strong.

SHAKUNI: Exactly. So where are you strong?

DURYODHANA: I have ninety-nine brothers! We can tear his head off this instant!

SHAKUNI: My nephew. If you want to be a king, then you must start thinking like a king. Violence is rudimentary and primitive. A good king takes the unexpected path – that way victory lies.

DURYODHANA: When I am king I'll build an army and smash Bhima to pieces.

SHAKUNI: Bhima is built like an elephant, and it is rumoured that he and his brothers are born of gods! Violence will activate his strength. You need to think about where he is weak. It is there where your power lies.

DURYODHANA: Bhima has a wolf-belly. He will devour anything that's put in front of him … I'll prepare Bhima a feast!

SHAKUNI: Ah, yes, my nephew. The best way to kill an enemy is with friendship.

DURYODHANA: But inside the spicy snacks and luscious sweetmeats that he loves, I'll smear a deadly poison, enough to kill him ten times over. Then, once he's weak, I'll bind him and –

STORYTELLER: Splash!

Bhima is held in suspension, as if he is underwater.

Bhima sinks to the bottom of the river. Revenge. Revenge was something that Shakuni was reminded of every time he limped. Many years ago, Shakuni's father –

Flashback.

SHAKUNI'S FATHER: Bhishma! No! Bhishma, please forgive us.

BHISHMA: *(to Shakuni's father)* You have brought dishonour upon my family. I will starve out the wickedness in you and all your sons.

STORYTELLER: Bhishma locked Shakuni's father and brothers in a dungeon, and every day he sent only one fistful of rice to eat.

SHAKUNI'S FATHER: This is not enough for all to survive. Let only Shakuni eat. Let him grow to be strong and to take vengeance for us all!

STORYTELLER: Only Shakuni ate the rice while the rest of his family starved, his brothers' eyes following his hand to his mouth with each bite.

SHAKUNI: Father, I will make Bhishma and his entire family pay for what he has done to us, I swear!

SHAKUNI'S FATHER: Son, take my bones and make them into dice; they will be filled with my rage and will turn whichever way you want them to.

STORYTELLER: Before dying, his father struck Shakuni's foot with a staff.

SHAKUNI'S FATHER: Now you will limp every time you walk.

STORYTELLER AS SHAKUNI'S FATHER: And when you limp, remember the crime Bhishma did to our family. Never forgive him.

Music and lighting take us out of the flashback and we return to the present scene.

STORYTELLER: Bhima has been at the bottom of the river for eight days. His body is swarmed by scarlet and green serpents who sink their fangs into his limbs. Their venom is the antidote to Duryodhana's poison.

Bhima comes back to life and bursts out of the water.

SCENE 16: DRONA AND DRUPADA BACKSTORY

STORYTELLER: Year by year, as the princes grow, Bhishma oversees their education. They study history, the science of statecraft, and how wealth is created. But as young Kshatriya princes, they measure themselves by their prowess in the arts of warfare. It just so happened that around that time a very special person was arriving in Hastinapura, an old friend of Bhishma's: Drona, Master of War.

BHISHMA: Drona, my friend, you seem rather troubled.

DRONA: Bhishma, I came here seething with a great obsession. When I was young, I had an unlikely friendship with a young prince, Drupada, who had been sent to study with my father in our humble home in the forest. He became so dear to me, and I to him – we were inseparable. We spent everyday together; often we fell asleep in the same bed, hating to put an end to conversation. We were more than friends, we were brothers, and he promised me ...

Drupada enters as if in Drona's memory. Bhishma does not see him, but Drona hears his voice.

YOUNG DRUPADA: Drona, when I am king of Panchala, you shall live in the palace with me, and you shall share all of my wealth.

DRONA: Not long ago, I fell on times of crippling poverty. I was too poor even to buy milk for my young son, Ashwatthama. I thought of Drupada, and of our friendship, and I decided to go to Panchala where Drupada now is king. I travelled for days and arrived collapsing with exhaustion, ragged and half-starved. I asked to see the king, telling the guard my full name, confident that my old friend Drupada would hurry out to greet me. But that's not how it was. Two days he kept me waiting by the gate, despised and ridiculed by passersby. At last, I was conducted to his presence, where he sat, bejewelled, lolling at ease upon his ivory throne. I greeted him, 'My old friend Drupada!

DRUPADA: Scruffy brahmin, how dare you presume to call me friend! Of course, we knew each other when we were boys, but that was another life. Friendship is a bond between equals, and in those days your friendship suited me. But did you delude yourself we could remain eternal boys, alike in innocence, forever irresponsible, outside time?

No: time and circumstance change everything. With time comes experience; with circumstance comes the parting of ways. We are not equal, we never were, nor shall we ever be.

Drupada exits.

DRONA: It was as if an icy hand clutched and twisted my heart. My eyes struggled to penetrate the scarlet mist that swirled in front of them. Only revenge can free me from the rage and hurt I carry!

BHISHMA: Drona, my friend, please stay here with us. You are exactly the teacher our young princes need. Here you will be honoured as you deserve. It seems to me destiny has sent you.

SCENE 17: TRAINING

Arjuna, Bhima, Yudhishthira, and Duryodhana train as Drona watches them. The movement is inspired by the Indian martial art kalaripayattu.

STORYTELLER: Drona was a most exacting master, demanding discipline from all his pupils.

The training sequence ends. The boys each take a knee, as Drona instructs.

DRONA: Boys, I have placed a small wooden bird high up in this tree. Take your bow, aim. Yudhishthira, tell me everything you see.

YUDHISHTHIRA: Everything?

DRONA: Yes.

YUDHISHTHIRA: I see the clouds in the sky, the branches of the tree, the tip of my arrow …

DRONA: Back to your place. Duryodhana, Bhima, aim. Tell me what you see. Bhima!

BHIMA: Guruji, I see the bird and the tree, I see my bow …

DRONA: What else?

BHIMA: I see my brothers, and I see you.

DRONA: Duryodhana?

DURYODHANA: I see the top of the tree, my bow, the wooden bird.

DRONA: Sit down. Both of you! Arjuna, take your bow. What do you see?

ARJUNA: I see the bird's eye. Nothing more.

DRONA: Do you see the tree?

Arjuna is silent in concentration.

The sky?

ARJUNA: Only the eye.

DRONA: Release your arrow.

Arjuna's arrow hits the bird.

STORYTELLER: Arjuna was extraordinary. He was tall, quick moving, and his skill with the bow and arrow was unlike anything Drona had ever seen. Drona saw in Arjuna the solution to his problem.

DRONA: Arjuna, I shall do all in my power to see that you become the greatest archer in the whole world. This I promise you.

SCENE 18: EKALAVYA

Drona begins to train Arjuna in private. The music shifts as Ekalavya enters, and through a dance sequence he travels around the circle as if making the journey to Drona. Ekalavya arrives and speaks to Drona while Arjuna is training on his own in deep meditation.

STORYTELLER: Drona's renown as a Master in the Arts of War spread throughout the kingdom and beyond.

EKALAVYA: Dronacharya, I travelled from the other side of the world to receive your teaching. Train me, guruji.

DRONA: Who are you?

EKALAVYA: My name is Ekalavya, and my father is the chief of the forest people.

DRONA: Ekalavya, my lessons are reserved for the elite. I teach only youths who have come from highborn families.

EKALAVYA: How will I learn if you don't train me?

DRONA: If you have faith in me, you'll teach yourself.

Ekalavya shifts to a different time and we see him moulding the form of Drona.

STORYTELLER: Ekalavya runs home and scoops up clay from the river's edge and carefully models a life-size figure of Drona. It takes him days and nights of work. And when it is complete, Ekalavya gathers perfumed flowers and makes a garland for his master's neck. Then, under Drona's watchful gaze, Ekalavya begins to practise with faith, devotion, and pure discipline.

Ekalavya does a pranam and begins to train. He works in slow motion as the focus returns to Drona and Arjuna.

ARJUNA: I can see in the dark. Guruji, last night as I was eating by candle-light, a sudden gust of wind blew out the flame. I continued to eat, and in the darkness my hand still found its way to each dish in front of me, unerringly. So I ran out into the moonless night, flexed my bow, knocked an arrow, and though the target was invisible I found the arrow clinched in the exact place I had intended. I can see in the dark!

STORYTELLER: Arjuna was indeed becoming the greatest archer in the world.

Ekalavya returns to real-time and performs a virtuosic feat with his own arrows.

ARJUNA: Who are you and where did you learn to shoot like that?

EKALAVYA: My name is Ekalavya, and I owe my skill to the great Drona, my master.

ARJUNA: Guruji! How can you secretly teach this lowborn boy? He makes me look like a mere beginner!

DRONA: I am not your teacher.

EKALAVYA: Guruji, yes you are. For years I have trained under your watchful gaze.

ARJUNA: Drona, did you not promise that you would make me the greatest archer in the world?

DRONA: Ekalavya, if I am your teacher, you should now give me my fee.

EKALAVYA: Name it – anything! There is no gift I shall withhold from you.

DRONA: Give me your right thumb.

STORYTELLER: Ekalavya's smile does not falter. He slices off his right thumb and places it, dripping, at Drona's feet. Drona's words will not be falsified: Arjuna will be the greatest archer in the world.

Lights fade slowly on the scene, lingering on Drona and Arjuna before going to black.

SCENE 19: GRADUATION CEREMONY

STORYTELLER: I take you now to an enormous amphitheatre. Excited crowds have gathered from small towns, villages, and fishing settlements. Because the young princes have completed their training, and now all their years of effort will be crowned by a grand demonstration of their skills. Conches blare, drums beat out a tattoo, the cry goes up: 'AR-JU-NA, AR-JU-NA!' He is the warrior they've all come to see. They stomp their feet, chanting in ecstasy, the entire stadium vibrating.

Arjuna strides forward in complete concentration. He raises his bow, draws back an arrow, and then the miracles begin. First he sends an effortless stream of arrows into the mouth of a tiny boar, so far off it's almost out of sight. Not one arrow misses. Then he does the same again, blindfolded. Then again with his back turned. It looks impossible.

Now Arjuna stands with his eyes closed, his lips moving in a silent mantra. He shoots one arrow into the ground and it cracks open in front of him. When he walks inside, the ground closes behind him and the earth begins to tremble. Just as people are beginning to worry, a crack opens up in front of the royal stand, and Arjuna pops out and bows before his uncle. The crowd goes wild!

BHISHMA: My king, young Arjuna is the greatest archer Hastinapura has ever seen!

Karna enters through the audience.

KARNA: Pandava! You seem to take great pride in the facile feats you've displayed.

DHRITARASHTRA: Bhishma, who is here?

BHISHMA: A man as tall as a kadamba tree …

GANDHARI: What does he look like?

BHISHMA: He wears a shining golden chest plate and two golden earrings, like two drops of sunlight hanging from his face …

DHRITARASHTRA: Stranger, who are you and why have you come here?

KARNA: King Dhritarashtra, with your permission, I will now match each paltry trick that Arjuna has just performed and show the world who truly is the greatest archer.

ARJUNA: The great Drona is my master. Who is yours?

Silence.

BHISHMA: This is a royal hall, you cannot come here unannounced –

DHRITARASHTRA: Where are you from? Are you of royal birth?

DURYODHANA: What difference does it make? Father, surely he should be given the chance to prove himself before we judge.

Pause.

DHRITARASHTRA: Very well, I will allow him to compete with Arjuna in a demonstration of skill.

BHISHMA: But King –

DURYODHANA: May the best archer win!

Through a physical sequence, Karna and Arjuna compete, revealing that Karna is the more skilled archer.

DURYODHANA: Welcome to you, strong-armed hero! Hastinapura is honoured by your presence. What is your name?

KARNA: Karna.

DURYODHANA: Karna, from today, the kingdom of Hastinapura is home to you. Ask of me what you will.

KARNA: Prince Duryodhana, I ask only two things of you: your life-long friendship and a duel with Arjuna.

KUNTI: Wait!
It is known that no prince will condescend to duel with a man of lesser lineage than his own. Here stands Arjuna, third-born son of this royal house. You must tell us, hero, who your father is. Who is your mother?

KARNA: I do not know. My mother abandoned me; a chariot driver found me and raised me.

Bhima laughs.

DURYODHANA: This rigmarole is just old-fashioned nonsense! If Kunti is too punctilious to allow Arjuna to fight with anyone except a prince, I have the solution. Our vassal state, Anga, lacks a ruler. Here and now I propose that this outstanding man shall be consecrated King of Anga. Then there will be no excuse for Arjuna not to duel with him. Father, bless this man!

Silence.

DHRITARASHTRA: Karna, you have my blessing.

DURYODHANA: Karna, King of Anga.

The crowd reacts.

KARNA: King of Anga?
Duryodhana, brother, here is my promise: as long as I shall live, while these two arms have strength and skill in them, I shall defend you.

BHIMA: King? This man is no king, he is a wagoner's son! Off with you, off to the stables – go and muck out the horses. That's where you belong!

DURYODHANA: Wolf-belly, your rudeness and crass ignorance are hardly worthy of the prince you claim to be. The learned scriptures distinguish three kinds of king: one of a royal line, the leader of an army, and a hero. Karna, by his heroic skill, his courage, has proven himself equal to any of us. As for his origins, why should it matter? The most powerful forces in the world are often born in darkness. The mightiest rivers have unimpressive origins; their greatness grows as they make their journey through the world. That's how it is with the noblest warriors.

But, of course, a deer can't sire a tiger, and this man is a tiger. So I would guess his mysterious birth must hold a clue to his greatness. Karna deserves –

The crowd interrupts.

– hear me out – our deep respect and, in my eyes at least, he is a king. Now, Bhima, tell your little brother to gather his scattered wits, pick up his bow, and fight the King of Anga – if he dares!

KARNA: I will not cut off my thumb for you.

ARJUNA: I swear to you, when I have killed you, you will sink to the realm of those who indulge in empty boastful prattling!

KARNA: Strength is what matters here, not whimpering words, not half-baked insults. I, Karna, challenge you to a contest – no mere display, but a duel to the death between archers. I shall behead you in your mother's presence.

ARJUNA: I accept.

STORYTELLER: As they speak, the sky grows dark. Indra, Bringer of Storms, is gathering his forces to bless his son, Arjuna. The next moment a shaft of brilliant sunlight pierces through the clouds, creating a golden circle around Karna. Kunti faints!

SCENE 20: KARNA

Flashback to Karna's birth.

STORYTELLER: Who was this extraordinary youth who dared to challenge Arjuna?

The tune of the same lullaby from Karna's birth is heard, and we see flashes from Kunti's dance: his birth, her placing the baby in the river, Kunti walking away. We are left with Karna alone onstage.

STORYTELLER: Karna was abandoned. The river carried him into the arms of a kind chariot driver and his wife, who loved him and gave him a humble home. But the mystery of his birth made him feel like a stranger in his own skin. Karna always felt that he was destined for something greater, something just out of reach.

Karna kneels before Parashurama.

KARNA: Parashurama! You are the most formidable weapons teacher in the world. It was you who trained the great Drona, Master of War. I beg you, accept me as your pupil.

PARASHURAMA: I do not train warriors of high status.

KARNA: Master, I am a lowly charioteer, I am no warrior.

Parashurama accepts him.

STORYTELLER: From him, Karna learned all the weapons of the gods that Arjuna had mastered, and more!

PARASHURAMA: Karna, you are unbeatable. Your genius with the bow far surpasses that of any pupil I have known – but remember, these sacred powers must be used in the service of dharma. Death is the price for using them for any evil purpose.

STORYTELLER: One day, his master was feeling tired, so Karna made a pillow of his lap, and his master slept. Suddenly Karna felt a piercing pain: a worm was burrowing into his thigh.

Karna suffers silently, until finally his master wakes up, discovering the blood that has dripped onto his face.

PARASHURAMA: What is this? Blood?

KARNA: I did not want to wake you!

PARASHURAMA: How can you tolerate pain so agonizing? Have you lied to me? You are not the son of a charioteer, your blood is that of a warrior!

KARNA: Master, I am the son of a charioteer – I have not lied! My birth is unknown to me …

PARASHURAMA: Your selfish ambition is at the root of this. One day, when your very life depends on it, and you try to invoke the godly weapons I have taught you, your memory will fail. That is the day that you will meet your death.

Parashurama exits, Karna is alone. Arjuna enters and they lock eyes and counter each other around the circle of red dirt as the Storyteller narrates the next line.

STORYTELLER: From that day on, Karna walked through the world alone; he knew his destiny could not be bargained with, and yet his seething hatred for Arjuna festered. He was drawn to Arjuna like a moth to a flame, unaware that his greatest enemy was his younger brother … the favoured pupil of Drona.

SCENE 21: CAPTURE OF DRUPADA
AND CHILDREN OF SHIVA

Arjuna kneels at Drona's feet.

DRONA: Arjuna, your education is now complete. You are no longer a boy, you have become a man.

ARJUNA: Guruji, how can I ever repay you?

DRONA: You know my grievance against King Drupada. Year by year, the craving for revenge has swelled in me. This will be your fee: you shall take an army to Drupada's kingdom and bring him to me as a prisoner.

ARJUNA: I will do this.

STORYTELLER: And he does.

Music swells as Drupada is dragged in, his hands and mouth bound, and thrown at Drona's feet.

DRONA: My old friend Drupada. You once said friendship was impossible except among equals. Remember what you said? 'Time and circumstance change everything.' How right you were! You were the king but now you are defeated, and your entire kingdom is mine, given to me by my disciple as my fee. Your very life is mine if I should choose to take it. Instead I choose forgiveness. I'll make you my equal by giving half the kingdom back to you. Half is yours. Half is mine. As equals, the two of us may be friends again.

Drona and Arjuna leave.

DRUPADA: When we were young and played games, I let you win, knowing that you were always beneath me. No matter what you have stolen, we will never be equal. There is no such thing as equal!

STORYTELLER: Burning with rage, Drupada lights a fire and prays to Shiva, God of Destruction, for three children.

A song invokes Lord Shiva. Drupada performs the birth of the children as a dance. As he dances, he moves around the circle, destroying the perimeter. His dance scatters red dirt in all directions. We see the images of his children arise through his dance: Dhrishtadyumna, who will behead Drona in the war to come; Shikhandi, who is a reincarnation of Amba; and Draupadi, who has been born to save the earth with Krishna. As the dance becomes more frenzied and the circle is destroyed more and more, a large circular disc, lit up at the edges, slowly descends from the sky. The dance increases in tempo and intensity as Drupada spins. As the music finishes, Drupada comes to an immediate stillness. He performs the mudra for Shiva. Curtain.

ॐ

INTERMISSION

ACT 3: GODS

SCENE 22: STORYTELLER AND JANAMEJAYA

The curtains rise, and the stage has been transformed. The circle of stools no longer exists. Instead, a carpet has been laid over the destroyed dirt circle at the centre of the stage. Upstage centre of the carpet is a large throne, where Dhritarashtra sits, with Gandhari and Shakuni on each side of him. The ensemble is now divided on either side of the carpet, sitting on clusters of stools. The large circular disc is suspended halfway above the stage, and the ropes still hang behind the musicians. The Storyteller stands downstage centre, holding a bowl of fire, which she places at the lip of the stage.

STORYTELLER: Janamejaya and the storyteller sit by the fire. Janamejaya whispers, 'I will avenge my innocent father.'

'What do you see, my king?'

'I see thousands of devious snakes waiting to meet their fate.'

'My king, how do we end the cycles of revenge where both sides believe they are right and the other wrong?'

The question rolls around the back of Janamejaya's head. As his neck cranes back, he sees thousands of snakes hanging in the air. Their eyes twinkling in the firelight. Their lives suspended in numerous stories within the *Mahabharata*.

'Where were we?' says the king.

Having defeated King Drupada, the Pandavas had acquired a taste for battle. They began going on campaigns, growing their lands, expanding their kingdom, and earning a most glorious reputation.

The wealth and power of the Bharatas was largely due to their father, Pandu, who had been an outstanding warrior and beloved king, and young Yudhishthira resembled his father. He was generous, concerned for the people and their families, and the population loved him.

Dhritarashtra was constantly told of the Pandavas' prowess and strength, and he became filled with anxiety. His nights were sleepless and uneasy.

SCENE 23: THE PEOPLES' WHISPERS

Lights rise on Dhritarashtra, Gandhari, and Shakuni. The area covered by carpet now becomes the playing space of the palace, the perimeter outside (covered in dirt) becomes the forest.

SHAKUNI: King Dhritarashtra, my servants have heard whispers in their villages. The people believe the eldest Pandava, Yudhishthira, is wise beyond his years. They want him to be king instead of you.

GANDHARI: I am afraid that I have heard the same. The people are saying that because of your blindness you did not inherit the throne; they are asking, 'Why are you king now? Why should your son inherit the crown?'

DHRITARASHTRA: Those same voices swirl in my head.

SHAKUNI: Dhritarashtra, every day the Pandavas are nourished by the people's love for them. This will make it impossible for your Duryodhana to inherit the throne.

GANDHARI: It was you who gave the Pandavas strength when you welcomed them back into the palace.

DHRITARASHTRA: Bhishma says that dharma is for the mighty to protect the meek, this is our duty.

GANDHARI: Yes, but those Pandava cubs you took in, fed, and protected have grown into hungry lions, and now we are the lambs. Arjuna single-handedly captured the mighty Drupada. Bhima sneezes and armies fall. Yudhishthira's honesty is unmatched, and the people see their future under his reign.

SHAKUNI: She's right, your nephews are becoming dangerous. You have been kind to the Pandavas too long, giving them more light while Duryodhana has suffered in their shadows.

GANDHARI: Duryodhana is in anguish, and for good cause. The love you have for your son, it is not shared beyond the palace walls.

SHAKUNI: Duryodhana is not trusted.

GANDHARI: All living creatures call for the most honest of men, the son of Dharma, Yudhishthira.

DHRITARASHTRA: My heart is wracked with uncertainty. What can I do?

SHAKUNI: You must be bold; a king should strike against his enemies before they grow in power.

DHRITARASHTRA: The Pandavas are not our enemies. They are our nephews. They are our sons.

GANDHARI: By treating the Pandavas like your sons you have allowed Yudhishthira to usurp the place that Duryodhana should occupy in popular esteem.

DHRITARASHTRA: What can we do?

SHAKUNI: I have a plan, at least to give you some breathing space –

DHRITARASHTRA: Yes, what is it?

SHAKUNI: Send the Pandavas away on some journey. In their absence, we will build our public base. We will do what it takes for Duryodhana to become popular in order to support his claim to the throne. The people's memories are short and fickle. Once they start receiving generous handouts, they'll switch support to him.

DHRITARASHTRA: But what about Bhishma? Would he not understand this plan as a banishment?

SHAKUNI: Banishment?! No, my lord, we will give them time to travel, rest, and be loved! Send the Pandavas on a royal tour to Varanavata. There, there is a festival in honour of Lord Shiva. And as a gift to the Pandavas, you should build a palace filled with every luxury so they will feel honoured and celebrated and spend enough time there for Duryodhana to build his base here.

DHRITARASHTRA: The plan is perfect and will remove the dreadful thorn that's sticking in my heart. You may go.

SHAKUNI: My king, my queen.

Shakuni makes as if to leave but silently lingers at the edge of the room, listening to the following conversation.

DHRITARASHTRA: Gandhari?

GANDHARI: Yes?

DHRITARASHTRA: My queen, have I done well?

GANDHARI: What choice do we have? There are two contestants to the throne but only one with the people's hearts.

DHRITARASHTRA: Do you think the people could learn to love Duryodhana?

Gandhari is silent.

A king who is not loved by his people sits on a hollow throne.

GANDHARI: We must give Duryodhana a chance! You know he cannot compete with the Pandavas. So long as they are here, he will never be free.

DHRITARASHTRA: Gandhari, you believe the sons of my brother Pandu are our sons, yes?

GANDHARI: I do. And yet …

DHRITARASHTRA: In your heart you have a preference.

GANDHARI: The same as you.

Dhritarashtra is silent.

And when one prefers one's own children to the children of others, war is near.

SCENE 24: THE LACQUER HOUSE

Duryodhana rushes in looking for his uncle.

DURYODHANA: Shakuni, Uncle, there you are! Will my father make me the king?

SHAKUNI: The choice is not his. If the people choose Yudhishthira, then your father will have no choice but to support him or there will be a revolution.

DURYODHANA: Does he realize he has condemned his own children to penury? If Yudhishthira becomes king, our family will be disinherited forever.

Karna enters.

KARNA: The Pandavas are being sent away to Varanavata. Let us go on glorious campaigns of our own – you will have time to win the love of the people!

DURYODHANA: Am I to hand out sweets!? Shake hands? Kiss babies to win people's hearts? Ha. The people's love – I shouldn't need the people's love, I am the rightful heir to the throne!

KARNA: Then let them see how great you are, earn their respect!

DURYODHANA: As long as the Pandavas are alive, they will always have the upper hand.

SHAKUNI: You need a more permanent solution.

DURYODHANA: Yes, we need to burn the Pandavas out of the people's memory …

The Storyteller takes focus as Duryodhana, Shakuni, and Karna leave to make a plan.

STORYTELLER: Duryodhana sends his men ahead to Varanavata, to the house that his father is building in honour of the Pandavas. He instructs his men to stuff the walls with straw drenched in oil and to wax the floors with twenty coats of lacquer. The entire house is a tinderbox, waiting to be lit.

Cut to the Pandavas and Kunti arriving at the house. They are at the perimeter of the carpet; they know that something is amiss.

YUDHISHTHIRA: Do you smell that?

ARJUNA: It's a trap.

BHIMA: Yudhishthira, we must leave at once –

YUDHISHTHIRA: No, we cannot betray the slightest gesture that we have noticed anything. Our cunning must equal his.

KUNTI: It's true. If we should show that we have realized what Duryodhana is plotting, he will have us followed and killed.

YUDHISHTHIRA: We must be patient and discreet.

STORYTELLER: The plan was simple: give the Pandavas time to settle in, enjoy themselves without suspicion, and then, one windy night, when everyone was asleep …

The Storyteller lights a match and drops it in the bowl stage left.

The entire house went up in flames. The people of the town gathered, helpless. 'Shiva! Shiva! A fire consumes the house where the Pandavas slept … the Pandavas are dead!'

Scandal erupts throughout the kingdom. Rumour and conspiracy blaze in people's hearts and minds.

Bhishma rushes to find Yudhishtira safely hiding in the forest.

BHISHMA: Everyone believes you're dead. King Dhritarashtra has cast off his royal robes and declared public mourning, kingdom-wide. They carry out the proper funeral rites, worthy of kings.

YUDHISHTHIRA: Grandfather, I burn with rage, I want revenge!

BHISHMA: Anger is not strength but rather weakness. Do not let it guide you.

YUDHISHTHIRA: What justice is there, if we who are wise and virtuous hide here, filthy and emaciated, and allow Duryodhana to take our kingdom?

BHISHMA: The day will come when you will sit on the throne, but it will not come easily.

YUDHISHTHIRA: Why should we run like hunted animals when we should be living in the palace? I should be king. We must tell everyone the truth and reveal Duryodhana's plan to kill us.

BHISHMA: Dhritarashtra and Gandhari are blind to Duryodhana's intentions. They will not believe you.

YUDHISHTHIRA: But it is the truth.

BHISHMA: My son, power determines truth. Duryodhana has keys to the treasury, political advisors, an army; he is the heir apparent –

YUDHISHTHIRA: But the people cry out for me to be king! If we go back with the people behind us, we will –

BHISHMA: Start a revolution and divide the kingdom even further.

YUDHISHTHIRA: So what are we to do?

BHISHMA: Remain in hiding. You have no land, no army, no power. First you must get married. Establish your own kingdom and make yourselves kings.

YUDHISHTHIRA: Bhishma, Pitamaha, why is it, if these plants can coexist in harmony, that we cannot live side by side with our cousins?

BHISHMA: You don't share the same truth, and when the truth cannot be agreed upon, war is inevitable.

SCENE 25: KRISHNA'S ARRIVAL

STORYTELLER: Three gods rule the universe, three who are also one. Brahma, the Creator, who is indefinable, unknowable. It was Brahma who birthed the universe into being. Shiva, the Destroyer, who takes on many forms. At the end of each cosmic age, the dancing Shiva, surrounded by flames, will consume the earth. The third god is Vishnu, the Preserver. It is Vishnu who maintains the worlds, who sustains us all. When the earth is threatened by chaos, Vishnu takes on an avatar and descends among us to play his role. In our story, he arrives as Krishna. If we had more time I would tell you all the stories of his incredible feats.

Krishna enters, listening in on the Storyteller.

KRISHNA: No, please.

STORYTELLER: Of the mountain he held on one finger.

KRISHNA: Don't, don't – I'm right here.

STORYTELLER: Of the terrifying disc that comes when he calls it and can destroy everything.

KRISHNA: You mean this? I'm only joking. Tell them about the one with my mom and the dirt.

STORYTELLER: Once, when he was a child, he was outside playing and he started eating dirt –

KRISHNA: Kids!

STORYTELLER: When his mother asked him to open his mouth, she saw the entire universe turning inside it.

KRISHNA: Who knew?

STORYTELLER: He is the essence of everything that is. He is everywhere, all the time, all at once. He is the heat of fire, the roar of the wind ... he is the heart of all that is invisible. And he arrives at the swayamvara of Princess Draupadi, daughter of King Drupada. Princes from across the land line up to compete for her hand.

SCENE 26: DRAUPADI'S SWAYAMVARA

DRAUPADI: The task is this: there is a bow. There are five arrows. Overhead is a revolving wheel and, higher still, a target. Whoever strings the bow and hits the target through the wheel will be my husband. Which one of you is brave enough to try? Who will be first?

DURYODHANA: I will!

DRAUPADI: Prince Duryodhana, what a brave man you are.

Duryodhana strides forward and tries to lift the bow but it doesn't move.

DRAUPADI: Ha! He can't even lift the bow, let alone string it! I will never be queen to such a weak king.

STORYTELLER: Prince after prince makes an attempt but fails. They try to bend the bow, but it springs back and they limp away, sore, angry, ashamed ...

DRAUPADI: Oh men and their pride, how humiliating!

KARNA: I can do it.

DRAUPADI: Karna! You are no king.

KARNA: I am, I am the King of Anga!

DRAUPADI: No, you're not. Karna, you are the son of a charioteer, unworthy of my hand. I would never take you as my husband. Sit back down. That's right, like my little puppy!

KARNA: Draupadi, I swear that one day I will humiliate you as you have done to me.

DRAUPADI: Sit, Karna, sit! Is there no one who can begin to bend the bow?

Arjuna stands, a shawl covering his face, and slowly walks towards Draupadi.

STORYTELLER: Suddenly, a hooded figure –

DRAUPADI: With the stature of a god –

STORYTELLER: Strides forward. The stranger raises the bow –

DRAUPADI: With ease –

STORYTELLER: Strings it, and –

DRAUPADI: Effortlessly –

STORYTELLER: Shoots five arrows through the wheel –

DRAUPADI: And hits each target.

SCENE 27: THE DESIGN OF THE GODS

Draupadi pulls back the scarf revealing Arjuna's face.

DRAUPADI: There only is one archer in the world who can shoot like that! You must be Arjuna. But how can this be?

KRISHNA: The world is mourning at the Pandavas' funeral, and yet here we are celebrating their wedding!

DRAUPADI: Are you Krishna? Is it really you?

KRISHNA: Who else would it be?

DRAUPADI: I've heard stories of you. Why have you come?

KRISHNA: Sadly, my friend, I heard the Earth complain to Brahma.

YUDHISHTHIRA: What did she say?

KRISHNA: She said, 'Men live like gods, they despise moderation; ravaging me, they multiply, plundering the beautiful resources that are my gifts. They have abandoned dharma, oppressing and slaughtering gentler creatures so that life becomes misery.'

DRAUPADI: I have heard her in my dreams as well …

ARJUNA: She speaks to you?

KRISHNA: She does.

DRAUPADI: Krishna, is that why I am here?

KRISHNA: You and I have come into this world for the same reason, Draupadi: to be an instrument for the deliverance of the suffering earth, to carry out our part in the design of the gods. You are to be the palm that connects the five –

Bhima enters with Kunti, covering her eyes.

BHIMA: Mother, guess what Arjuna has won!

KUNTI: Whatever it is, my dears, you must share it equally between you.

Bhima uncovers Kunti's eyes, revealing Draupadi.

But how are they to share Draupadi without breaching dharma?

KRISHNA: Yet, if they don't, your words will be a lie.

DRAUPADI: This was your prophecy, Krishna?

KRISHNA: Draupadi, if you agree, you will be a queen to all five Pandavas.

DRAUPADI: I see before me many heroes, each wonderful in their own way. I trust the gods have given me a mysterious blessing.

KRISHNA: Draupadi, you will be the palm that connects the five Pandavas, and preserve the earth.

DRAUPADI: The Earth says she shall be destroyed.

YUDHISHTHIRA: What can save her?

DRAUPADI: A king who will re-establish dharma.

KRISHNA: A king who will be calm and just. Without him, the Earth is lost.

YUDHISHTHIRA: Am I this king?

KRISHNA: Yes.

YUDHISHTHIRA: What must I do now?

KRISHNA: Shed your anger, return to Hastinapura, and tell everyone that you are alive.

KUNTI: Krishna, will the Kauravas give my sons the throne of Hastinapura?

KRISHNA: No, but there is another way.

BHIMA: We have our queen, we have land –

ARJUNA: We have the people's support –

DRAUPADI: And my father, the mighty Drupada, will put his entire army in your service.

YUDHISHTHIRA: Our youth is over. We will go to the king and let all know that we are alive.

ACT 4: ILLUSION

SCENE 28: DIVIDING THE KINGDOM

Cut to Duryodhana, Karna, and Shakuni.

DURYODHANA: Alive? The Pandavas are alive?!

SHAKUNI: This disaster could eliminate you.

KARNA: Somehow, they managed to escape the fire, and now you are the objects of suspicion.

DURYODHANA: The Pandavas must also suspect us. Why else have they been in hiding so long? They will waltz back into Hastinapura just as they did so many years ago and ruin my life again!

SHAKUNI: Only this time they come with their bride, Draupadi, and her father's formidable army.

KARNA: Let us defeat them in open battle – that is the most honourable way.

Dhritarashtra and Bhishma enter.

DHRITARASHTRA: Such wonderful news that I have heard today! My beloved nephews, the Pandavas, are alive and well. What a triumph for the Bharatas!

BHISHMA: The time has come for us to right the wrongs of the past.

DHRITARASHTRA: My son, the Pandavas have suffered for too long. It is time for us to make peace and give the sons of Pandu their birthright. I have decided to divide the kingdom equally.

Dhritarashtra places a hand on Duryodhana's shoulder. Duroydhana shakes it off and walks away from his father.

KARNA: King Dhritarashtra, may I speak?

BHISHMA: No.

DHRITARASHTRA: Yes. Speak, Karna.

KARNA: The law says that the sole right to this kingdom belongs to the king's first-born son. You are the king of Hastinapura, and Duryodhana is your first-born. After you, he should be the sole king. This is the truth and the law.

BHISHMA: Yudhishthira is the eldest Bharata Prince; there is no question, he is the rightful heir.

KARNA: But King Dhritarashtra is the first-born grandchild of Satyavati.

DURYODHANA: The whole kingdom belongs to our family, and no part of it, nothing, belongs to the Pandavas.

BHISHMA: Duryodhana, listen: the people blame you for the fire of Varanavata, they suspect you for the attempted murder of your cousins! This is now your chance to return to the path of dharma and to redeem yourself in the people's eyes. If you respect dharma, oh Prince, relinquish half the kingdom.

KARNA: You speak the language of morality, but you are guided by your love for the Pandavas.

BHISHMA: How dare you!

KARNA: Duryodhana is my friend, and I have seen him to be loyal, wise, and kind. He was born to be the rightful king, as were you, King Dhritarashtra, only you were denied. They said a blind man could not be the king. But oh, Royal Dhritarashtra, you have proved they are all wrong! You have ruled with a wise and respected hand. Let Duryodhana prove everyone wrong too. Division is not a solution –

BHISHMA: The son of a driver thinks his opinion matters!

KARNA: This plan is a sludgy compromise; Bhishma has always favoured the Pandavas!

DHRITARASHTRA: Leave us!

Shakuni, Karna, and Bhishma leave.

DHRITARASHTRA: Duryodhana, what do you think of this plan?

DURYODHANA: Father, the people of Hastinapura are one people, our people as of right, bequeathed to us by our ancestors. Now you want half of them to bow to Yudhishthira as their lord? If you divide the land, families will be split, communities will grow apart, our people will suffer.

DHRITARASHTRA: As king you can choose to live in harmony, side by side, each governing your own kingdom.

DURYODHANA: The choice for harmony will not be mine. If you do this, the choice will belong to the people. Everyone loves the Pandavas, they want them to rule the whole kingdom. Not me, not you! This is your fault. If you were a strong king, we wouldn't have to heed the people's views.

DHRITARASHTRA: We sent the Pandavas away in order to build your popularity, and what did you do?

It's because of you the Pandavas are stronger, it's because of you the people's love for them grew in their death and ten times more with the news that they are alive! This plan will ensure there is at least half a crown in your future.

DURYODHANA: It will have disastrous consequences for the future generations.

DHRITARASHTRA: And that will be your burden to bear! You have left me with no choice. Tomorrow you will welcome your cousins with open arms.

DURYODHANA: But –

DHRITARASHTRA: Enough! The people of this kingdom will see that there is peace in this family!

SCENE 29: THE PANDAVAS ACQUIRE A KINGDOM

STORYTELLER: The Pandavas return from the dead! The city has never seen such celebration. Every gate and arch is garlanded. The pathways are strewn with lotus petals, and the people flood the streets, careening over each other, trying to catch a glimpse of the Pandavas' royal return.

The Pandavas and Draupadi arrive at the palace, kneeling before King Dhritarashtra. Bhishma, Karna, and Duryodhana are with him.

DHRITARASHTRA: Welcome! Welcome home to the Pandavas. This indeed is a great day – my beloved nephews alive and well! My sons, for you are all my sons, it brings me joy and relief to know we are together. And now blessed with a new daughter, Draupadi. I wish my brother Pandu had lived to see this day. Yudhishthira, the prosperity of our noble kingdom owes a great deal to your father, Pandu, and to you, of course. Yet, to my sorrow, you and Duryodhana are constantly in conflict with each other. I have decided to put an end to all this disagreement: the kingdom will be split in half exactly. I will continue to rule Hastinapura as king until such time as Prince Duryodhana takes on the burden of the monarchy. Yudhishthira will be a king at once, as he deserves. He will rule the other half of the kingdom from Khandavaprastha.

YUDHISHTHIRA: Uncle, we humbly accept this gracious gift.

BHISHMA: May peace prevail between these kingdoms.

BHIMA: No, Khandavaprastha is a barren region, a wasteland of dry brush and dense forest. It is no place for royalty.

DURYODHANA: It is a great forest full of birds and beasts; you will fit right in.

BHIMA: I swear to you, Duryodhana –

YUDHISHTHIRA: *(interrupting Bhima)* Silence, Bhima. We accept and thank you, Uncle.

Cut to Pandavas outside in private.

BHIMA: Why do you accept their charity like a beggar?

ARJUNA: This is banishment.

YUDHISHTHIRA: We will agree to this plan with dignity.

BHIMA: Dignity?! We are kings, and yet we live like animals.

YUDHISHTHIRA: There is no future for us in Hastinapura. We will build a palace of our own and draw the world to us.

SCENE 30: BURNING OF THE KHANDAVA FOREST

STORYTELLER: The Khandava Forest. Huge old trees that tower upward; cool, deep ponds; rich soil covered in fungi. It is a mysterious place: thousands of beings living in harmony with each other in a complex web of relationships that has developed over millennia. And Krishna tells Arjuna to burn down the entire forest in order to feed the god Agni. So Arjuna does.

Takshaka, the snake, sticks out his tongue, and is the first of all the animals to taste the smoke from Arjuna's arrow. As he looks around, he sees the lush green wither as the smoke and flames grow closer.

Suddenly, a terrible screeching starts. Animals scattering mindlessly. Mothers and fathers trying to save their children, while mates cling together, unable to abandon one another. Takshaka watches entire families and tribes meet death together.

He watches as Arjuna and Krishna hunt down any animals that try to escape.

When he looks up, he sees birds bursting into flames before they can meet cooler air. He sees fish and tortoises jumping out of boiling ponds, only to burn and suffocate in the thick smoke.

Terrified, Takshaka burrows himself deep down into the earth. Days later, he emerges to find a wasteland, black ash dancing in the air, the ghosts of trees. He is alone. The last survivor of the massacre, the only survivor of his family and his entire race.

As he watches the figure of Arjuna disappear into the distance, he swears he will have vengeance on Arjuna and his descendants for what has been done to his family.

SCENE 31: BUILDING THE PALACE OF ILLUSIONS

The huge disc that hangs in the air is lowered to the ground.

STORYTELLER: From the ashes of the fire, a city emerges, which the Pandavas name Indraprastha, and people from all corners of the earth flock to it. At the centre of the city, a palace is built for the Pandavas that is the embodiment of cosmic harmony, inviting visitors to be alert and to reflect on the nature of illusion.

Krishna instructs Yudhishthira to perform a ritual that will make him the emperor of all the lands. A sacred fire is lit, and the ceremony begins. Priests pour water, milk, and honey on Yudhishthira's head, as kings take turns lining up and bowing before Yudhishthira, offering cascades of wealth at his feet: gold, jewels, pearls, a glittering stream pouring into the royal coffers. Yudhishthira is crowned King of Kings.

SCENE 32: DURYODHANA FALLS INTO A POND

Duryodhana, Gandhari, and Dhritarashtra are in the palace at Hastinapura. Shakuni lurks behind and eavesdrops. As Duryodhana describes the Palace of Illusions, subtle projections flash, revealing the circular disc as a projection surface.

DURYODHANA: A coronation beyond imagining!

DHRITARASHTRA: Come now, Duryodhana.

DURYODHANA: I cannot bear it.

DHRITARASHTRA: The sons of Kunti deserve prosperity!

DURYODHANA: I stood in their great hall and watched the whole world flock to honour Yudhishthira as king and the radiant Draupadi as queen. The Pandavas have made heaven on earth, all from nothing. And I, who have fought so hard to simply inherit my father's throne, I am nothing!

GANDHARI: You are so much more!

DURYODHANA: The way those kings looked at me. Their pitying eyes … their sickly polite smiles … Laughing at me … Even the palace mocked me – it is full of illusions, full of tricks! Marble that looks like water, ponds so still that they seem like stone, painted roses asking to be picked. Arjuna walks through a door and I follow and bump my head on the wall! There is no door. It vanishes. The servants laugh. I plunge into a deep pool that I took for crystal, I'm soaking wet. Bhima howls like a hyena! I tumble through arches, taking them for painted walls. Draupadi whispers, 'Blind father, blind son.'

Oh I am sick with humiliation. Seeing the Pandavas ensconced as emperors of the earth and wallowing in wealth is agony.

GANDHARI: My son, the gods are on their side – jealousy is useless. You must not despair.

DURYODHANA: What man, knowing that such success is beyond his reach, would not despair?

GANDHARI: You must find happiness with what you have. You have every luxury, the finest clothes, the swiftest horses. As our eldest son, you will inherit half the kingdom!

DURYODHANA: Why should I be content with half when I should rule the whole kingdom? By law it should all be mine. Mother, in giving them half, you have given away everything. My future as the king is gone. The Pandavas grow their armies, they grow their support, they grow their half. It is only a matter of time until they will come for mine.

SCENE 33: SHAKUNI'S PLAN

Shakuni, who has been listening this whole time, enters the room.

SHAKUNI: Yes …

GANDHARI: Shakuni, is that you?

SHAKUNI: Yes, sister.

GANDHARI: Brother, what do you think?

SHAKUNI: Your son is right. We must be clever or else a war is inevitable.

DHRITARASHTRA: What do you suggest?

SHAKUNI: There is a way for the Pandavas to return their half of the kingdom to you, willingly.

DURYODHANA: They would never do that.

SHAKUNI: Invite Yudhishthira to the traditional game of dice.

GANDHARI: But he's a terrible gambler.

SHAKUNI: And yet he loves to play. Yudhishthira cannot refuse a game. I will play on Duryodhana's behalf, and with these dice our father gave to me, I will win all his wealth from him.

DHRITARASHTRA: I seek the advice of Bhishma.

DURYODHANA: He would never allow it.

SHAKUNI: A game of dice is the only way to take the wealth of the Pandavas without the loss of blood on either side. The dice will be my arrows, the board my battlefield, my hand the chariot that will lead our family to victory.

DURYODHANA: Father, this is not just for me, this is for the future of our family. Can you not understand that?

GANDHARI: Greed and envy are dangerous – there is only one path they lead man to.

DURYODHANA: Discontent and jealousy are good for humanity! Content-ment weakens the ambition, so does fear, and so does limp compassion. In pursuit of prosperity, any means, any means at all, are justified.

GANDHARI: Peace must be attained by any means.

DURYODHANA: Peace?! Mother, I saw the most respected kings from across the land wait in line to shower an abundance of gifts on Yudhishthira. To honour him. Did any of them come to pay respects to you? Our halls, which used to greet those same kings, are now empty.
  How much more are you both willing to lose in the name of peace?

DHRITARASHTRA: Dice-playing is a noble pastime … No harm need come of it.

GANDHARI: Extend an invitation to Yudhishthira.

DHRITARASHTRA: Fate will have its way. Let fortune be bestowed where the gods decide.

Dhritarashtra stands, as if the following were an invitation being sent to the Pandavas.

Come, my dearest nephews, honour Hastinapura with a visit. A splen-did gaming hall is being built where you will be entertained at dice.

Yudhishthira is alone.

YUDHISHTHIRA: A trap is waiting for me. And yet it is my duty to obey the wishes of my uncle. I am honour-bound, and bound by my own vow not to refuse a challenge. But what man is there who is not subject to the blinding power of fate that dazzles us, depriving us of reason? What will happen is what time ordains.

STORYTELLER: Yudhishthira accepts the invitation.

SCENE 34: THE GAMBLING MATCH

The stage is transformed. A row of chandeliers descends slowly from the ceiling, The disc is raised to hang above Dhritarashtra's throne. The Pandavas and Kauravas meet in the hall.

YUDHISHTHIRA: Who will play against me?

DURYODHANA: Shakuni will play on my behalf. I put my entire wealth at his disposal.

YUDHISHTHIRA: Shakuni, you have never lost a match. I trust you will play fair and not win by trickery.

SHAKUNI: We are all in the hands of destiny. Let the play commence!

YUDHISHTHIRA: I stake my pearls, sourced from the depths of the ocean.

DURYODHANA: I match.

They play.

SHAKUNI: I have won.

YUDHISHTHIRA: I stake five hundred chests bursting with pure gold!

DURYODHANA: I match.

They play.

SHAKUNI: Look, I have won.

YUDHISHTHIRA: I stake my army, well-trained, and a thousand rutting elephants.

DURYODHANA: I match.

They play.

SHAKUNI: I have won.

They play three quick rounds.

SHAKUNI: I win again!

YUDHISHTHIRA: You confuse me with a trick.

SHAKUNI: In playing dice, the stronger player tries to defeat the weaker. What you call trick, I call skill.

BHISHMA: King Dhritarashtra, surely this game has gone on long enough.

DHRITARASHTRA: Yudhishthira is free; he may leave the game at any point he wishes.

DURYODHANA: King Yudhishthira, are you afraid? Will you walk away from the challenge?

YUDHISHTHIRA: I have vowed never to refuse a challenge. I stake my part of the sacred River Ganga –

BHIMA: Brother!

YUDHISHTHIRA: Lined with fruit-bearing trees, abundant with fish of all kinds.

DURYODHANA: I match.

We are no longer in realistic time. The ensemble performs a rhythmic clapping sequence each time the dice are rolled, as Yudhishthira and Shakuni play round after round.

SHAKUNI: I have won.

They play.

I have won.

They play.

I have won.

They play.

I have won.

They play.

I have won his treasury, his palaces, lands, and his entire kingdom of Indraprastha. I have won it all!

DURYODHANA: Have you nothing more? Surely your luck will turn – you could win back everything you've lost.

ARJUNA: Brother, walk away.

YUDHISHTHIRA: No! Again! We will play again!

BHISHMA: Oh, wise king, I beg you: reconsider what you have set in train. When Duryodhana was born, the jackals cried, an ill-omened howling that echoed through the palace; it echoes still. I told you he was sure to bring destruction to the Bharatas. You would not listen then. Now, see what he is doing.

DURYODHANA: You have always been partial to the Pandavas, and yet you stay around here, like a cat scratching spitefully at those who feed it. You should get lost, old man.

SHAKUNI: Have you nothing more?

YUDHISHTHIRA: My brothers. I stake my brothers: Nakula, Sahadeva, Bhima, Arjuna.

They play.

SHAKUNI: I have won! Look, I have won his brothers. It seems they are dispensable to him.

YUDHISHTHIRA: Wretch! Never try to put a knife blade between us. The five of us are of one heart, one soul. Let us play again!

SHAKUNI: King Dhritarashtra, it seems emotions have overcome our great King Yudhishthira. Perhaps it is best to heed Bhishma's advice and allow the game to end?

YUDHISHTHIRA: NO! I am still unwon, still free to leave this hall. I hereby stake myself!

They play.

SHAKUNI: I have won.

DURYODHANA: Yes! We have won everything! You are all my slaves.

KARNA: Yudhishthira, all is not lost, you can still win back everything. There remains one asset dear to you: your wife, Draupadi.

DURYODHANA: Yes, by staking her, you could win back yourself.

ARJUNA: You jackal, how dare you?

YUDHISHTHIRA: She who is perfect, neither too tall nor too short, whose eyes sparkle with love –

BHIMA: Brother! Wake up!

YUDHISHTHIRA: Whose care for us is boundless –

ARJUNA: Bhishma! Please!

YUDHISHTHIRA: Our matchless Draupadi – I stake her.

They play.

STORYTELLER AS SHAKUNI: I have won!

STORYTELLER: A messenger is sent to Draupadi's chamber.

STORYTELLER AS MESSENGER: Oh queen, you are summoned to the hall. King Yudhishthira has lost his reason and has gambled away every one of his possessions: city, wealth, kingdom, his brothers, himself, and, madam, you.

DRAUPADI: Go back and ask my husband if he gambled me before he lost himself, or afterward. Then come tell me.

STORYTELLER: Draupadi is dragged by the hair into the gambling hall.

SCENE 35: THE DISROBING OF DRAUPADI

DURYODHANA: Come, my fine girl. You have been lost at dice and are nothing but a slave. We own you now. You'll have to learn to love the Kauravas and show us how you've made our cousins so happy!

DRAUPADI: It is an outrage for you to drag me here by the hair into a hall of men! You are all well-versed in dharma – and yet not one of you raises your voice at this disgraceful insult. Do you lack courage? Or do you condone this vile behaviour? A curse on you! My husbands will not pardon this offence.

DURYODHANA: You will speak when you are spoken to –

DRAUPADI: King Dhritarashtra, did my husband gamble me before he lost himself or after?

Silence.

When he put me up as his last stake, he had already gambled himself away into slavery, is that not so?

KARNA: Draupadi, notice, no one here is speaking up to say you have not been won. Accept it.
Now you will be my pet; come eat from my hand!

DURYODHANA: You are all slaves now, you own nothing, even the clothes on your back belong to me. I want your clothes.

The Pandavas concede, taking off their jewellery and shawls and leaving them on the floor. Draupadi watches them.

Draupadi, I'm waiting. Strip her.

One of Duryodhana's brothers pulls at one end of Draupadi's sari. Draupadi closes her eyes and speaks a mantra, a prayer to Krishna. Her robes are endless; it is magical.

BHISHMA: King Dhritarashtra, a miracle is happening before us … Her robes are endless.

DRAUPADI: The Gods have stood up when men would not! Lords of the earth, where is honour in this hall? Where is dharma? Time must be out of joint when such outrages can be enacted unprovoked, unchallenged.

I am the wife of the great Yudhishthira, equal to him in rank. I am the daughter of King Drupada, and the friend of Krishna.

I ask again for an answer to my question – am I won or not?

DURYODHANA: The Kauravas are your masters now. Choose another husband, one who will not gamble you away – or shall we share you?

A jackal begins to howl.

DHRITARASHTRA: Duryodhana, you have gone too far. This day will bring disaster to this house! Virtuous Draupadi, please forgive me, I am an old fool. Ask me for a boon and you shall have it.

DRAUPADI: Free Yudhishthira from servitude.

DHRITARASHTRA: Let it be so. Now ask again. Let me grant you a second boon.

DRAUPADI: Let my other husbands go, let them be free.

DHRITARASHTRA: It shall be as you say. Now, ask again for a third –

DRAUPADI: These two boons are enough for me. Greed is a threat to virtue.

DHRITARASHTRA: You are all free. Go now in peace and bear no grudge against us.

KARNA: In Draupadi, these cowards have a boat ferrying them across to their salvation.

BHIMA: As the gods are my witnesses, I vow, Duryodhana, that before I enter the halls of death, I will tear open your wicked breast and drink your blood.

The Pandavas leave.

SCENE 36: THE FINAL MATCH

DURYODHANA: Father, what have you done?! You think that by freeing them we can go back to the way things were?

Dhritarashtra is silent.

The Pandavas will never forget how Draupadi was insulted.

Dhritarashtra is silent.

You think you are making peace, but in restoring their freedom, you have started a war. Summon Yudhishthira to play again!

BHISHMA: Surely it is fathers who should dictate to sons, not the reverse.

DHRITARASHTRA: If fate decrees the ruin of our race, I cannot oppose it. One more game. Let the Pandavas return!

Dhritarashtra sits on his throne, Bhishma by his side, while the Storyteller narrates the final story to the audience, but also to Dhritarashtra. We hear the voices of the characters when they speak.

STORYTELLER: A message is sent. The offer is extended. And the Pandavas return to the hall one last time. Duryodhana says:

DURYODHANA: Just one throw each, and let the stake be this: that whoever loses will relinquish their kingdom to the other. For twelve years that loser will be exiled in the forest, the thirteenth year is to be spent in public, incognito. If he is recognized, another twelve years of exile will commence. If he succeeds in hiding his identity, then, at the end of thirteen years, his kingdom will be returned to him.

STORYTELLER: They roll the dice …

SHAKUNI: I have won!

STORYTELLER: Duryodhana rejoices, slapping his thigh. Bhima curses him.

BHIMA: You stupid fool.
 I vow, Duryodhana, in the great battle to come, I will tear your ninety-nine brothers limb from limb, I will break that thigh of yours, and on that day you will plummet into the deepest, darkest pit of Death!

STORYTELLER: Arjuna turns to his rival.

ARJUNA: Karna, more certain than the sun's brightness, more certain than the moon's coldness, is this vow of mine, that thirteen years from now, I will dispatch you, son of a charioteer, to the realm of Death.

STORYTELLER: Draupadi rages.

DRAUPADI: I will keep my hair unbound until I wash it in Kaurava blood.

DRAUPADI/STORYTELLER: As I am stained with blood today, so, thirteen years from now, Kaurava women will be smeared with the blood of their slaughtered sons.

STORYTELLER: They leave the palace. As they walk through the city, crowds of grieving people line the streets. Yudhishthira drapes his shawl across his face. Draupadi rages. Bhima strides with his massive arms outspread. Arjuna scatters sand, each grain standing for an enemy he will one day strike down. They disappear into the distance.

DHRITARASHTRA: I can only think of the future and its terrible punishment. Bhishma, I fear my great love for my son will bring about the all-consuming tragedy of war.

  And yet, all things done cannot be undone. We must live with what will be.

STORYTELLER: The storyteller turns to King Janamejaya. Do you hear that thumping in the distance, my king? Your ancestors are dancing toward their deaths.

The Pandavas and Kauravas stand on either side of the carpet, each facing their rivals. Dhritarashtra and Bhishma sit at the throne. Music swells. The Storyteller looks up at the disc that glows above the throne and raises her hand, conducting the final note of the band's music. Blackout.

INTERLUDE
KHANA AND KAHANI
A COMMUNITY MEAL

ACT 5: KHANA AND KAHANI

Khana and Kahani is a community meal that takes place between Part 1: Karma *and* Part 2: Dharma. *After leaving the theatre, audiences are invited to eat a South Asian meal and experience one story from the* Mahabharata *around the dinner table. The audience eats their meal seated at tables around a centre platform. On the platform, a small table is set with Miriam and Sharada sitting facing one another.*

MIRIAM: Hey, everyone! Welcome to Khana and Kahani. I'm Miriam, and I am one of the writers of the show, along with Ravi, who directed the show. Please keep eating while we talk, be comfortable – we want you to feel at home while you're here. My grandma used to say that stories are the business of life and the dining room table is the meeting place to do our business, so welcome to our table.

So, I didn't really grow up with this story. It was kinda in the background of my life, but nobody really told it to me. I got pieces of it through a television series or comic books, and every now and then, I would catch a story at a family gathering. The one story that I remember is the one where Krishna was a child and he was eating mud and his mom made him open his mouth, and when he opened his mouth, inside she saw the entire universe. And it stuck with me because it was like a mirror – I used to eat mud as a kid, and I wasn't a god, but I had a universe in my head, of stories ... and I became a storyteller. So in coming back to the *Mahabharata* as an adult, and trying to figure out how to shape an experience for an audience, I wanted to bring us back to the feeling I had as a kid being at those family gatherings.

It is rare for someone to sit and listen to the entire *Mahabharata* from beginning to end; most people receive one story at a time, often around a meal where you learn not only the story but also the meaning hidden within. And most often the story is told by an elder, an auntie or uncle –

SHARADA: Excuse me! I am not an auntie!

MIRIAM: Ha! Of course *you're* not an auntie!

SHARADA: I'm your didi.

MIRIAM: *Didi* – it means older sister in Hindi. (She's not actually my sister.)

SHARADA: But in Indian culture we're all related.

MIRIAM: Right. So my didi, Sharada, is a writer and a storyteller, and she is the person I learned the stories of *Mahabharata* from. Over the past many years of writing this adaptation, Sharada has been the person I've gone to whenever I'm feeling lost, because she's a great storyteller, and today, she is also an actor!

SHARADA: No, no, no, I'm not an actor!

MIRIAM: But for now I've *forced* you to be an actor – just for today – because I wanted the audience to experience one of the many conversations we've had over meals talking about *Mahabharata*.

SHARADA: Okay, but I'm not someone who can memorize lines!

MIRIAM: That's okay – like any good story, we'll pretend. We'll pretend that we're sitting in your kitchen, and that there are no scripts in front of us. *(to the audience)* And if you can't see one of our faces, pretend you can.

SHARADA: Can we pretend I cooked the food too? It smells so good!

MIRIAM: Of course! So, here we are, at your kitchen table, we're all sharing a meal and taking a moment to digest this epic, the same way you and I have been doing for many years …

SHARADA: Okay, so I'll start by saying I have a bone to pick with you!

MIRIAM: I thought it was a vegetarian meal!?

SHARADA: Haha. Very funny. No! I saw *Karma*, and it was really great, I loved it – but you left out so many great stories!

MIRIAM: I know …

SHARADA: You didn't tell the story of Sisupala and Krishna's Sudarshana Chakra!

MIRIAM: That is a great one …

SHARADA: And Vidura, you completely cut out the character of Vidura!

MIRIAM: We didn't have the budget for another actor. But seriously, there's a lot of story to tell! Give us a bit of credit, at least we got to the game of dice –

SHARADA: Yes, okay, and I quite like the way you did that with all that clapping! Fancy.

MIRIAM: And now the Pandavas are going into exile in the forest for thirteen years.

SHARADA: Oh great! Are you going to tell the story of how Bhima goes searching for lotuses and is humbled by Hanuman?

MIRIAM: No …

SHARADA: What about the time Arjuna visited Indra's abode?

MIRIAM: Uh-uh.

SHARADA: No? What about the story of Draupadi and her akshayapatra?

MIRIAM: Sharada, we have to fast-forward a lot, there's so much story to tell!

SHARADA: Please, please, tell me you are telling the Yaksha story!

MIRIAM: Yes, that's the one we're gonna tell tonight.

SHARADA: Uff! Thank god! I was going to ask for my money back. You have definitely redeemed yourself. The Yaksha story, that's a good one! My grandmother used to tell us that one over lunch.

MIRIAM: *(to audience)* Oh, this is a great story! You should tell them!

SHARADA: Oh yes. My grandmother was an amazing storyteller and an even more amazing cook. She would gather all the grandchildren around her in a semi-circle and preside over us with her own akshayapatra of leftover food. She would then ask us to stretch out our little hands and, going around the circle, she would place the most delicious balls of food into the cups of our palms, all the while telling us this story. The end of the story would always mean the end of the food. Perfect timing!

MIRIAM: No leftovers!

SHARADA: Yep. She was a smart woman, my grandmother.

MIRIAM: Well, they're all eating. So shall I tell the Yaksha story?

SHARADA: Sure, be my guest. Why not? See what I did there? You are Why Not Theatre? … Get it? Never mind!

MIRIAM: Oof, Sharada, you're moving from didi to auntie territory very fast!

SHARADA: Whatever!

MIRIAM: Okay, so the Pandavas lose the game of dice. They are sentenced to twelve years in exile in the forest, and a thirteenth year in hiding, where, if they are discovered, they have to repeat twelve more years in exile. So they leave the palace and wander through the forest for twelve long years. On the eve of the thirteenth year, the eldest brother, Yudhishthira, has a dream: the Forest tells him that the Pandavas have been killing so many deer that they are throwing off the balance of nature. So the Forest tells Yudhishthira that he and his brother must leave.

When Yudhishthira wakes up, he realizes his youngest brother, Nakula, is missing.

Nakula has gone to fetch water from a nearby lake, and by the time he arrives, he is overcome with thirst, so he bends down to drink. As the water is about to touch his lips, Nakula hears a voice say, 'I am the Yaksha, lord of this lake. You may drink, but only after answering my questions.'

Nakula looks around and sees no one, so without heeding the words, he drinks the water cupped in his hands and he falls down dead at once.

Since Nakula never returns from the lake, Yudhishthira sends his twin, Sahadeva, to look for him. When Sahadeva arrives at the lake, he sees his brother dead on the ground and begins to cry. But soon he is overcome by the same thirst and in his desperation he does not heed the Yaksha's warning: 'You can drink only after answering my questions!' When the water touches his lips, he also falls down dead at once.

Next, Yudhishthira sends Arjuna, who is stunned to see his two brothers' bodies lying dead by the lake. But his desire to drink overpowers his sadness, and he too bends to drink. He also ignores the Yaksha's warning and drops dead instantly.

The same happens to Bhima.

When Yudhishthira finally arrives at the lake himself, he sees his four brothers lying dead on the ground. Dead. What could have happened?

Yudhishthira is also fatigued by thirst, and he decides to drink. Like his brothers before him, he hears a voice: 'I am the Yaksha, lord of this lake. You may drink after answering my questions.'

Unlike his brothers, Yudhishthira immediately drops the water and says, 'Are you the one who has killed my brothers?'

'Yes,' says the voice. 'They disregarded my warning. They did not answer my questions.'

Yudhishthira says, 'I shall answer your questions the best that I can.'

The Yaksha asks,

SHARADA: 'What makes the sun rise?'

MIRIAM: Yudhishthira answers, 'God.'

SHARADA: 'What makes the sun set?'

MIRIAM: 'It's the sun's natural duty, it's dharma.'

SHARADA: 'What is faster than the wind?'

MIRIAM: 'The mind.'

SHARADA: 'What is more numerous than grass?'

MIRIAM: 'Thoughts.'

SHARADA: 'What, when renounced, makes one agreeable?'

MIRIAM: 'Pride.'

SHARADA: 'What is the worst disease?'

MIRIAM: 'Greed.'

The last question Yaksha asks is –

SHARADA: 'What is the greatest wonder in the world?'

MIRIAM: Yudhishthira looks around, he sees his brothers dead on the ground at his feet, and he says, 'The greatest wonder is that every day creatures die, yet the rest go on living as if they are immortal.'

The Yaksha is greatly impressed by Yudhishthira's answers and says, 'I shall let one of your brothers live, who shall it be?'

Without hesitation, Yudhishthira says, 'Nakula.'

'Why? Why him, a half-brother? Why not Arjuna and Bhima, who are powerful warriors?'

Yudhishthira says, 'My father had two wives. I, the son of Kunti, am alive; surely a son of Madri must be kept alive too.'

Impressed by his sense of fair play, the Yaksha restores all four Pandavas to life. The Yaksha then reveals his true identity. He was none other than Yama, God of Death, also known as Dharma, Yudhishthira's father.

MIRIAM: *(turning back to Sharada)* How did I do?

SHARADA: Not bad. But you are focusing only on the plot! What about the meaning?

MIRIAM: The meaning comes from the plot, no?

SHARADA: Not exactly. I find the meaning comes with time. The more you visit and revisit these stories, the more their mysteries are revealed. You see, my grandmother used to say with the *Mahabharata*, 'Don't be confused by plots –

MIRIAM: Right, you said this to me. '*Within the forest of stories lies the wisdom of your ancestors.*'

SHARADA: And in this story, the wisdom being passed on is dharma. It is the thread that connects the entire epic. The epic is not about a gambling match, the disrobing of Draupadi, or the eighteen-day battle between the Pandavas and Kauravas. It's most certainly not about who won the war. It's about dharma. And the many conflicts that dharma poses – both internal and external. Dharma, which has not one but myriad definitions.

MIRIAM: Yes, I've read many. It could mean: righteousness, duty, honour ...

SHARADA: Justice, truth ... So if you look at the story, right from the beginning, there is a reference to dharma.

MIRIAM: Where?

SHARADA: Yudhishthira has a dream. And in his dream, the forest tells him the Pandavas have to leave because they have been hunting down the deer so much that it has thrown off the balance of nature – they've been taking more than they need.

MIRIAM: Because Bhima eats a lot?

SHARADA: Ha ha ha! Probably, yes! But that's the thing about humans: we are insatiable. In the jungle, it is the lion's dharma to hunt deer – but the lion takes only what it needs. It won't take more. But that's not the case with human beings. We are constantly taking, and worse, we take more than we give back.

MIRIAM: That's why Krishna comes down to earth in the story, right? The earth is being plundered and destroyed, so he comes down to restore balance, to restore dharma.

SHARADA: See, when the forest tells Yudhishthira to leave, he is being reminded that his dharma is to counter his instinct to take from nature and to find a way to restore its balance.

But look at Nakula, Sahadeva, Arjuna, and Bhima: what do they do when the Yaksha warns them? They ignore him. Would it have killed them to listen?

MIRIAM: Well, it certainly killed them not to listen! But come on, give 'em a break – they're thirsty! They're in the forest, they have nothing, they just want to drink water – is that a crime?

SHARADA: No, it is not a crime to drink water. But it is not dharma to take whatever you want when you want it, especially if it doesn't belong to you. That is arrogance. The Yaksha has clearly told them the lake belongs to him, he's the lord of the lake. They can't just grab things. They put their own needs before those of others, and it's that ego that separates us from our animal sistren. We are not animals.

MIRIAM: Fair. We can't live by the law of the jungle: survival of the fittest.

SHARADA: We are humans, we are capable of empathy. It is our responsibility and dharma to protect those smaller, weaker, less privileged than us.

MIRIAM: Okay, but in the story, it's not clear what is right and wrong.

SHARADA: Is it ever clear in life? One of the things I love about the Sanskrit language, there are no opposites – it's not 'right' vs. 'wrong.' There is only dharma, and adharma. It's like saying 'truth and untruth.' It's not truth and lie. It's not as black and white as that. They are two sides of the same coin.

MIRIAM: Dharma is a slippery fish.

SHARADA: I agree. It is the hill that characters in the epic are willing to die on. Its meaning shifts with the context in which it is invoked. Dharma, as the *Mahabharata* puts it, is *sukshma*, so subtle that it is almost elusive. What is 'right' depends on its context.

MIRIAM: So what is Yudhishthira's dharma in that moment, at the lake?

SHARADA: He has been taking from the forest for twelve years, so it's his dharma to protect the environment. That's also his job as a king.

MIRIAM: But he's in exile!

SHARADA: Yes, he's in exile, but he's still a king. And he has a duty not only toward human life, but also toward the plant kingdom, the animal kingdom, and the spiritual world. He has a duty to perform. Remember, duty is another interpretation of dharma.

MIRIAM: So he has a duty to all of those kingdoms simultaneously?

SHARADA: Of course! I mean, take each of us – every day there are different roles we play. I have a daughter, I have a husband, I have my mother, who lives with me. I have to make a choice. My mother wants to go to the temple, but my husband wants to see a show – I have to make a choice.

MIRIAM: So how do you decide?

SHARADA: I have to choose between the different dharmas I am faced with: my dharma toward my mother and my dharma toward my husband. Just because I take my mother to the temple does not make me a bad wife. It makes me a loyal daughter.

MIRIAM: Tell that to my husband, Sharada!

SHARADA: These are hard choices, but we have to reflect before we take action and deal with the consequences – that's what the story tells you.

MIRIAM: Okay, how would you decide if the choice was between your husband's cooking or your mom's?

SHARADA: My mom's! Are you kidding me!? Eswar can barely open a can of beans! Look, every single day, every single moment, you're making a choice. You have made a choice to write out our conversation and share it with this audience. And the people here have chosen to listen to us. That's the dharma of the audience.

MIRIAM: So dharma is a choice, actually.

SHARADA: Yes and no. It is a choice, yes – a choice to take an action or not. Dharma is *also* about perspective. It is making sure that you are making the right choice.

MIRIAM: So you have to reflect before taking action …

SHARADA: Always! You have to think. Think before you act.

MIRIAM: And even that's hard – because in my mind I can justify a lot!

SHARADA: Like, let me ask you, if the Yaksha asked you what is the worst disease, what would you say?

MIRIAM: I would say hate.

SHARADA: I would have said ego. Yudhishthira said greed. It's not about getting it right, it's about taking the time to reflect and respond.
    It's all contextual – like even everything I'm saying now, you turned it into a script, but that was my perspective in *that* moment; now, some three years later, I have a very different point of view!

MIRIAM: I know. But we didn't have time to do the rewrite – it would be a whole other play!

SHARADA: My entire life, my relationship to each story within the *Mahabharata*, has changed as I've grown. The pursuit of the question is more important than the answer. That's the beauty of it; it keeps us listening and more open to new ways of understanding …

MIRIAM: Yeah, it makes space for our answers to change over time … That's the wonder of it – everything shifts.

SHARADA: And then there is this lovely moment, the final question: what is the greatest wonder?

MIRIAM: The greatest wonder is that every day, creatures –

SHARADA: Every day, creatures die, yet the living go on as if immortal. For me that's a WOW moment. And that was 4,000 years ago! You see, what I'm wondering is: when will we listen? How do we receive this ancient wisdom, let it …

MIRIAM: Change us?

SHARADA: Free us. You ask that question in the first part of the play how do we end the cycles of revenge where everyone thinks they're right and the other wrong? Can we free ourselves from revenge, greed, desire, the need to own land?

MIRIAM: Which is the perfect transition to Part 2, which we've called *Dharma* – and the war that's coming …

SHARADA: I look forward to it. I hear you have lots of projections!

MIRIAM: Yeah, it was really expensive. Any advice going into Part 2?

SHARADA: Ohh … I don't know … Do you remember what I said to you and Ravi when you first started writing?

MIRIAM: No. That was a million years ago, Sharada.

SHARADA: As you go along through the journey, remember there is the story and there is the metaphor, the meaning. Give it time. But I can't go on any longer; like my grandma before me, I see your food is done. I've done my job!

MIRIAM: Thank you, didi. And thanks, everyone, for joining us around the table. See you at *Dharma*!

PART 2

DHARMA

THE LIFE WE CHOOSE

ACT 6: NEGOTIATIONS

SCENE I: REPRISE

The curtain rises on a luxurious modern interior, furnished with carpets, lamps, and chandeliers. The ruined circle of red dirt is visible under the carpets. A wall of television screens hang in front of the rope curtain, displaying a kaleidoscope of natural forms: fire, then the forest canopy. Cables overhead and on the floor connect broadcasting and playback devices throughout the room. Krishna sits at the head of a long war room table to the left. Sanjaya observes a bank of computer monitors on a desk at the right. The Storyteller is perched on a desk at the centre.

STORYTELLER: Janamejaya and the storyteller sit around the fire. King Janamejaya thinks about his great-grandfather Arjuna and the thirteen years he spent in exile from his own kingdom. The rage he must have felt …

By now the sun has set and the evening air is cool.

With snakes still hanging suspended over a burning fire that will consume their entire race, King Janamejaya eagerly awaits the next part of our story, the war. A great epic battle. Twinkling eyes all staring at the storyteller; the story holds lives in its teeth.

But how to tell the story of this war?

Dritarashtra enters, followed by Bhishma.

King Dhritarashtra wanders through the palace. Voices from the past echo in his head.

DURYODHANA: Just one throw each, and let the stake be this: that whoever loses will relinquish their kingdom to the other. For twelve years that loser will be exiled in the forest, the thirteenth year is to be spent in public, incognito. If he is recognized, another thirteen years of exile will commence. If he succeeds in hiding his identity, then at the end of thirteen years, his kingdom will be returned to him.

STORYTELLER: They roll the dice.

SHAKUNI: I have won!

STORYTELLER: Bhima –

BHIMA: You stupid fool.

I assure you, Duryodhana, in the great battle to come, I will tear your ninety-nine brothers limb from limb, I will break that thigh of yours, and that day you will plummet into the deepest, darkest pit of Death!

STORYTELLER: Arjuna –

ARJUNA: Karna, more certain than the sun's brightness, more certain than the moon's coldness, is this vow of mine, that thirteen years from now, I will dispatch you, son of a charioteer, to the realm of Death.

STORYTELLER: Draupadi –

DRAUPADI: I will keep my hair unbound until I wash it in Kaurava blood.

DRAUPADI/STORYTELLER: As I am stained with blood today, so, thirteen years from now, Kaurava women will be smeared with the blood of their slaughtered sons.

STORYTELLER: Thirteen years have passed.

SCENE 2: SUING FOR PEACE, PREPARING FOR WAR

The Pandavas in the forest.

DRAUPADI: It is time to reclaim what is rightfully ours.

YUDHISHTHIRA: Draupadi, it would be foolish to believe that Duryodhana would concede so easily.

ARJUNA: We have kept the terms of our covenant –

BHIMA: And have suffered in the forest for thirteen years.

ARJUNA: And now, Yudhishthira, you should be reinstated as the King of Indraprastha.

DRAUPADI: I have longed to see you return to your jewelled throne, dressed in rich silk, as the rightful king.

Cut to Dhritarashtra and Bhishma, in the palace.

BHISHMA: King Dhritarashtra, the Pandavas have suffered far more than they deserve. The time has come for them to return home.

DHRITARASHTRA: Duryodhana, with Karna, hunts for them. He is looking to reveal them, to prolong their exile.

BHISHMA: And you do nothing but wander through the palace from room to room.

DHRITARASHTRA: I am haunted by nightmares.

BHISHMA: You, my king, have treated your brother's sons cruelly and unjustly.

DHRITARASHTRA: I know! Every day for thirteen years, I have been haunted by the sound of rolling dice. Of Bhima's vow to tear my sons limb from limb. Of Draupadi's screams –

Duryodhana calls from offstage.

DURYODHANA: Father, I have found the Pandavas!

Karna and Duryodhana enter.

BHISHMA: You must guide Duryodhana to honour the terms of the agreement and return Indraprastha to the Pandavas.

DURYODHANA: The terms of our agreement were made clear: twelve years of exile and a thirteenth year in hiding, when, if found, they must live another thirteen years in the forest. And I have just found them!

BHISHMA: Nonsense.

KARNA: They are hiding as servants in King Virata's court. Though they are in disguise, they are unmistakable.

DURYODHANA: They say Arjuna has acquired weapons of the gods that can bring about the end of the world. We must expose them and return them to their exile.

BHISHMA: Dhritarashtra, this game has gone on long enough.

KARNA: By the solar calendar their thirteen years have not ended.

BHISHMA: By the lunar calendar, they have.

DURYODHANA: No, they have not!

BHISHMA: You must restore the Pandavas to their rightful kingdom.

DURYODHANA: Why should we return what was ours to begin with?

BHISHMA: Dhritarashtra, if you don't stop this now, then war is inevitable.

DHRITARASHTRA: War? No. We must avoid war at all costs.

DURYODHANA: I agree. Father, the choice is theirs: follow the rules and go back into exile, or if they will not, the Pandavas can choose war.

The Pandavas in the forest.

YUDHISHTHIRA: War? It would be better to beg in the streets than to go to war with our family. We must reach out and negotiate for peace.

BHIMA: Peace? Where was peace when Duryodhana set fire to our house in Varanavata? Where was peace when he left me to die at the bottom of a river?

DRAUPADI: Where was peace when I was gambled away, dragged by the hair, and stripped in a hall of men?

YUDHISHTHIRA: Will war bring you peace, Draupadi? Bhima? Do hundreds of thousands of people need to die for you to have your justice?

ARJUNA: Brother, Bhima and I possess the skill and strength we need to crush Duryodhana –

YUDHISHTHIRA: The path of dharma needs no violence, for the mighty must take care of the weak –

BHIMA: And if the mighty do not, the weak must prove their might.

YUDHISHTHIRA: Krishna –

Krishna appears.

You will be our envoy to the Kauravas. Tell them we do not want war –

ARJUNA: But that does not mean that we will opt for peace on despicable terms. Tell Duryodhana to ponder hard and well before he decides to break the covenant made thirteen years ago.

YUDHISHTHIRA: We want nothing more than what we were promised: our half of the kingdom returned to us. On this point, we are immovable.

SCENE 3: NEGOTIATIONS (PT. 1)

Throughout this sequence, the screens flicker with images of Shiva: his eyes opening, his feet dancing, spinning in circles.

KRISHNA: Wake, wake, great Shiva,
 Sing our destruction,
 That we gain new life …
 Open your three eyes,
 Lift your bow,
 Pound the world with your tread.

Krishna, Dhritarashtra, Karna, Duryodhana, Bhishma, and Drona all sit at the long table. Their faces are live-streamed on the television screens.

Sir, I bring greetings from Yudhishthira. He sends respects and prays for your good health. He wishes me to say he bears no grudge for what he and his family have suffered up to now.

I come here wishing to benefit both the Kauravas and the Pandavas, to bring peace.

The house of Bharata has been renowned for its courageous following of dharma, but now your sons, led by Duryodhana, have brought your great house into disrepute driven by greed. If you do not check him, catastrophe will follow – a war so terrible, both sides will be strewn, lifeless, on the field of battle. If you now follow the righteous course of action and return Indraprastha to the Pandavas, it will be for your good as well as theirs.

DHRITARASHTRA: You are right, but I cannot act alone. Speak to my son.

KRISHNA: Duryodhana, why wage what you know is an unlawful war?

DURYODHANA: You should ask that question to the Pandavas. They are the ones who dare attempt a coup!

KRISHNA: The Pandavas are your cousins. This is not 'a coup,' they are asking to return home.

DURYODHANA: They want to steal my land.

KARNA: And then gamble it all away again.

KRISHNA: How can you say that of your family? You know that is not true. You know Yudhishthira would not claim an inch of land, if he thought that claim was at all unlawful. Give your cousins back what is rightfully theirs. It is your duty.

DURYODHANA: My duty is to govern and protect my people; that is my dharma. If the Pandavas seize my land out of avarice, then it is my duty to go to war.

KRISHNA: What is dutiful and what is sinful is not straightforward. You took advantage of Yudhishthira and stripped the Pandavas of their kingdom.

KARNA: Yudhishthira came freely to the gambling hall and lost. He agreed to the terms of exile.

DURYODHANA: We have done nothing wrong.

KRISHNA: Nothing wrong? Do you think it is forgotten how you tried to burn the Pandavas alive, and how you subjected virtuous Draupadi to utter humiliation? You claim that you've done nothing wrong? Shame on you, Duryodhana!
Yudhishthira is entitled, as Pandu's heir, and as the first-born Bharata, to the whole kingdom. Nevertheless, he asks for only half.

DURYODHANA: Pandu never should have been king to begin with. My father was first-born, the rightful king, And I, as his son, am the rightful heir. He was denied kingship because he was born blind. I am simply here to restore our family's right. The hasty carve-up of the kingdom long ago was an ill-judged mistake.

KARNA: It never should have happened.

DURYODHANA: I was young and could not prevent it. Now I rule the entire kingdom for my father. The land is as it should be: one kingdom. That is how it will stay.

KRISHNA: Dhritarashtra, I call on you now to act – it is your duty. Bind the prince and his friend before they bring disaster on an unknown scale.

DHRITARASHTRA: Krishna, how can you ask me to choose between my sons and the sons of Pandu?

KRISHNA: Not long ago you believed they were all your sons.

DHRITARASHTRA: Duryodhana is flesh of my flesh – how can I abandon my own body to favour others?

Silence.

KRISHNA: Bhishma. Drona.

Silence.

Duryodhana, when you were born they said you'd bring about the ruin of our family.

DURYODHANA: Ruin? No, Krishna, I protect. As my mother protected me when I was born. As I protected Karna when no one else would. As I now protect my family and our kingdom. Our right from birth. I am not ruin, I am justice.

KRISHNA: Justice is an illusion; what you seek is revenge. You are attached to the past and cannot see that you have everything and the Pandavas have nothing. The law of dharma states –

DURYODHANA: They are breaking our agreement, Krishna. What does dharma say about those who break the law?

KRISHNA: What are the finite laws that govern men to the infinite laws that govern the universe?

DURYODHANA: I must ensure that laws are followed; if not, there is no civilization, only chaos and disorder.

KRISHNA: Poor Duryodhana, you only see what you want to.

DURYODHANA: I see perfectly well, Krishna, it is you who does not see –

KRISHNA: You promised to return Indraprastha after the Pandavas endured thirteen years of humiliating exile. They have kept their word.

DURYODHANA: No, they did not.

KRISHNA: You must keep yours.

DURYODHANA: No.

KRISHNA: For the sake of peace, give them at least five villages so that they may live with dignity.

DURYODHANA: No.

KRISHNA: Five houses in one village.

DURYODHANA: NO! Not even a needlepoint of land will I part with. Not while I'm alive. I'm ready to fight. If it comes to death, then heaven awaits me.

KRISHNA: You have destroyed the foundation of dharma. You must therefore be destroyed.

KARNA: How dare you threaten him?

DURYODHANA: Karna, arrest him!

KRISHNA: I wouldn't do that if I were you.

STORYTELLER: A blinding light. Krishna's body blazes fire. Weapons in his many hands. A gaping mouth. Nostrils flicker flames.
    A river. Sunset.

A bright light pulls focus to the Storyteller. The TV screens flicker, then settle on an image of Krishna's eyes. Everyone at the negotiation table is in suspension as if time has stopped.

SCENE 4: LOYAL FRIEND (KRISHNA/KARNA)

Krishna and Karna speak in another space and time.

KRISHNA: Karna.

KARNA: Krishna, I see you everywhere, in all your brilliance …

KRISHNA: Why do you fight for Duryodhana when you know he is wrong?

Silence.

See that bay there? That's where Adhiratha found you, a little baby, floating down the river. Karna, you have searched all your life to understand the mystery of your birth. What if I were to tell you that the men Duryodhana fights are your own brothers?

KARNA: I'd say it was an illusion.

KRISHNA: You are the first-born son of Kunti, conceived by Surya, the sun god. You are the eldest of the Pandavas. It is you who is the rightful heir to the throne.

KARNA: This is a trick to get me to quit the battle, to make me leave Duryodhana.

KRISHNA: You know in your heart that I speak the truth. Duryodhana cannot win without you. He would give up all thought of war if you changed sides. Come with me – your true brothers, the Pandavas, will embrace you, you will be king.

KARNA: Duryodhana has shown me nothing but love and loyalty; I will never abandon my friend.

KRISHNA: Karna, look at me.

KARNA: Kunti and the Pandavas have shown me only scorn and humiliation. How can you ask me to forgive? How can you ask me to love them?

KRISHNA: Karna, I am offering you the Earth.

KARNA: This revelation comes too late. Nothing – not gold, not offers of all the kingdoms in the world – could make me break my word to Duryodhana.

KRISHNA: Then my last hope is gone.

KARNA: Krishna, promise you will not reveal this secret to the Pandavas. If Yudhishthira knew I was his elder brother, he would resign his kingdom to me at once.

KRISHNA: If that happened, you would save the Earth.

KARNA: No. I would give everything to Duryodhana – I owe him any wealth and honour that I enjoy. I know full well that with your help the Pandavas will win. I can see it now, the dreadful bloodbath ... But I will not betray the Kauravas for whom I have pledged to die, if die I must.

Krishna leaves Karna, and walks toward Dhritarashtra, revealing his terrifying divine manifestation to the Blind King.

KRISHNA: Let there be war on the plains of Kurukshetra between the upholders of civilized conduct and the followers of the law of the jungle. Let the earth be drenched in the blood of those who do not deserve her bounty!

Krishna is gone. We are back in the Negotiations room.

SCENE 5: NEGOTIATIONS (PT. 2)

DHRITARASHTRA: Ah, Krishna, I see many gaping mouths and staring eyes, a million arms wielding divine weapons … I see a haunting vision of death and destruction. Bhishma, we must make one last offer of peace!

BHISHMA: It is too late; death is already here.

DRONA: The Pandavas are preparing for war.

DHRITARASHTRA: Drona, they will come to inform me of the death of my children and of my children's children. Call him back!

DURYODHANA: We are strong and we are ready. We need not fear. The Pandavas are only mortal men born / from human mothers, as we are.

BHISHMA: /They are the sons of gods with Krishna by their side.

DURYODHANA: Bhishma Pitamaha, with you, Guru Drona, and Karna leading our armies, our strength is unsurpassable.

KARNA: It's true: I know the weapons of the gods. Parashurama revealed them to me. I have vowed to kill Arjuna single-handedly; King Dhritarashtra, I will make this promise true.

BHISHMA: Duryodhana, my child, because of this lowborn companion, you have veered away from the path of dharma.

KARNA: You know nothing of who I am, Bhishma.

BHISHMA: You are a vain and boastful fool. How can you dream of killing Arjuna, the warrior who has never been defeated?

KARNA: Bhishma, you have always looked down on me, but the truth is, all this chaos is because of you, and your childish vow: never to marry, never to father children. You swore to protect this kingdom, and look what has become of it. Your words, like you, are impotent.

DRONA: Karna!

BHISHMA: There is no warrior who can defeat me, especially not the son of a driver.

DURYODHANA: Enough! Bhishma Pitamaha, I appoint you to be commander-in-chief of all my armies.

Pause.

You said so yourself: no one can defeat you.

KARNA: Why are you so afraid?

BHISHMA: Don't ask this of me.

DHRITARASHTRA: Bhishma, you made a vow that all your life you would protect the King of Hastinapura. If you lead, with Drona alongside you, my fears will be eased.

BHISHMA: You are asking me to kill my family.

DURYODHANA: I am asking you to save your family.

BHISHMA: I will be commander-in-chief, but on this condition: either I must fight first, or Karna must. The driver's son always seeks to rival me; I will not ride out with him.

DURYODHANA: No. We will fight together – we cannot win without him.

KARNA: Left to myself, I could destroy the army of the Pandavas in five days' time!

BHISHMA: You prove my point. You are rash and silly. Victory can never be achieved that easily.

DURYODHANA: Fine. If Bhishma is cut down, Karna will take up arms. Father?

DHRITARASHTRA: It has been decided. We are going to war.

SCENE 6: PANDAVAS DECIDE TO FIGHT

Cut to Bhima, Yudhishthira, Arjuna, and Draupadi in the forest.

YUDHISHTHIRA: How can it have come to this? It is as if no effort for peace has been made!

ARJUNA: We have tried everything. We sent Krishna! There is only one thing left to do –

YUDHISHTHIRA: No. There has to be another way.

BHIMA: You stay here in the forest then. I will not be banished from our kingdom. I will not have it stolen from us again!

YUDHISHTHIRA: Bhima!

BHIMA: Have you no fire in you, Yudhishthira? Why do you let them walk all over us? We cannot stand idly by again.

YUDHISHTHIRA: Is this dharma?

DRAUPADI: All this talk is driving me mad with grief!
      We know everything that we need to know. My strong husbands can trounce the Kauravas, but if you hanker pitifully after peace, then my father, Drupada, will fight, old as he is, and my brothers Dhrishtadyumna and Shikhandi will fight too! I've waited thirteen years for this precious moment – I want to see Karna chewing dust. I want Duryodhana to be dragged through the mud, his evil arms torn from his trunk for what he did to me: dragging me by this hair of mine, stripping me, reducing me to a naked slave. Every day, I relive those abuses and boil to think of how the Kauravas revel in luxury while we suffer in the forest!
      Thirteen years ago, you stood by, you did nothing. Do not repeat that mistake, Yudhishthira.
      There is no justice if a man like you – the very soul of dharma – accepts injustice. If you concede now, then might will govern everything and dharma is destroyed.

ARJUNA: They have given us no choice. We have to fight.

YUDHISHTHIRA: Krishna, have we done everything in our power to prevent this war?

KRISHNA: Absolutely everything.

YUDHISHTHIRA: Is there nothing more we can do to stop it?

KRISHNA: Perhaps ... if another war were to be fought.

YUDHISHTHIRA: Another war? With who?

KRISHNA: The question isn't who, but where?

YUDHISHTHIRA: Where? Where will this other war be fought?

KRISHNA: There are as many battlefields as there are people; the war is not outside, it is within.

YUDHISHTHIRA: Tell Duryodhana he will have his war.

SCENE 7: AMBA VISITS BHISHMA

STORYTELLER: At the start of Creation
There was a darkness without origin,
At the breaking of Creation
There is fire without end
As we inch toward the end of an age,
Shiva, God of Destruction, stirs.

Amba visits Bhishma as he prepares for battle.

AMBA: Bhishma, ease your worries. It will be over soon.

BHISHMA: Who are you?

AMBA: I draw closer and closer to you ...

BHISHMA: You haunt my dreams –

AMBA: I travel through lifetimes, through the infinite cycles of birth and death.

BHISHMA: What is your name?

AMBA: I promised never to eat, never to sleep, until I was the cause of your death.

BHISHMA: Amba.

AMBA: I am Amba. I leapt into fire seeking revenge in my next life. I was born from fire into the household of Drupada. And now, by the grace of Lord Shiva, I take part in this battle.

BHISHMA: What do they call you?

AMBA: My name is now Shikhandi.

BHISHMA: Shikhandi.

AMBA: I possess the frame of a man, but when you look upon me, you will see my heart beats as a woman. I will be the cause of your death.

BHISHMA: No one can kill me. I can choose the time of my own death.

AMBA: On the tenth day of war, I will return to you. When you see me, you will know me as the woman that I am. You will lay down your weapons in surrender.

She is gone. Conch shells blare.

SCENE 8: ONE SIDE OR ANOTHER

Duryodhana and Arjuna are waiting to speak with Krishna. Krishna stands with his back to them at a desk. When he turns, he sees Arjuna first.

DURYODHANA: Krishna, the entire kingdom marches toward Hastinapura. Each king must choose which side he will fight for. The time has come for you to pick a side.

KRISHNA: You are both close to me. I will give my support to each of you.

DURYODHANA: How can you be on both sides? Will you kill Kauravas one day and Pandavas the next?

KRISHNA: I have done all in my power to prevent this war. I will be present on the battlefield but will not fight.

DURYODHANA: What about your army? Who will they fight for?

KRISHNA: The choice that I will offer you is this: on one side, I offer an army of a million men, fully equipped and ready. And on the other side, I offer myself, alone, unarmed. Arjuna, choose first.

DURYODHANA: I was here first. Ask me what I want!

KRISHNA: Yes, you may have come first, but when I turned around, Arjuna was the first one I saw.

ARJUNA: Krishna, I choose to have you as my charioteer.

KRISHNA: Me, unarmed, vowing not to intervene. Are you sure?

ARJUNA: Yes.

DURYODHANA: Then it is settled. I will have Krishna's entire army. We will have eleven armies. You, Arjuna, have only seven. Victory will be ours.

Duryodhana exits.

ARJUNA: Krishna, we are outnumbered.

KRISHNA: Yes. But does it matter?

ARJUNA: Why do you offer Duryodhana your armies, knowing he is wrong?

KRISHNA: How am I to choose sides? This battle will be fought in the name of dharma.

ARJUNA: But to preserve civilization, those with the most power must take care of those with the least.

KRISHNA: You and Duryodhana are limited by finite power, and I, who am infinite? In front of me, you are both small. I shall consume you all.

ARJUNA: Krishna, what's the use of fighting if everything is to be destroyed?

SCENE 9: KUNTI AND GANDHARI

In the palace.

KUNTI: Open your eyes, Gandhari. Your son has launched a war against my sons.

GANDHARI: Duryodhana is protecting his kingdom.

KUNTI: Take off this blindfold – look at what he is doing! The field of Kurukshetra will be drenched in blood. Everywhere will be chaos, everywhere will be mangled flesh! Come out of your dark cave –

GANDHARI: To each one her darkness, Kunti.

KUNTI: All our sons will lie scattered on the earth, meat for undiscriminating crows.

GANDHARI: I cannot betray him.

KUNTI: You will sacrifice all for him? Think of each of your ninety-nine sons, think of each voice, each laugh, each embrace. You will let them all go to fight this senseless war?

GANDHARI: Kunti, for years we have tried to make peace between our children.

KUNTI: Duryodhana is bringing disaster, just as they said he would at his birth –

GANDHARI: No, these events are not preordained, and he alone has not chosen this war. If you want peace, tell Bhima to stand back, tell Draupadi to let go of her rage. They are hungry to crush the bones of my children into dust.

KUNTI: How did we get to this point? I ask myself every day: what could I have done to prevent this?

GANDHARI: Is it preventable?

KUNTI: I do not want any of our children to die.

GANDHARI: Nor do I.

KUNTI: Gandhari, you have been like a sister to me. I know it has not always been easy, but there has been love.

GANDHARI: Yes.

KUNTI: Open your eyes. Stop him.

GANDHARI: Kunti, how can a mother abandon her first-born?

KUNTI: If you don't, all will be destroyed.

GANDHARI: Even if you despise him, even if the Earth is afraid of him, he is my son.

SCENE 10: RULES OF WAR

The space is cleared of all furniture as soldiers are preparing the battlefield.

KRISHNA: Do you hear that thumping? The Earth is pulsing in anticipation as hundreds of thousands of warriors march toward the battlefield. Fathers say their goodbyes to their children, mothers pray to the gods to protect their sons, young boys clutching rings, amulets, necklaces – small pieces of the homes they may never see again.

Dhritarashtra approaches Krishna in the empty space.

DHRITARASHTRA: Krishna, I do not want war between my family.

KRISHNA: Wringing your hands is useless; time has run out.

DHRITARASHTRA: How am I to sit here while my children all are murdered? I know you have the power to stop the war.

KRISHNA: I only have the power to offer choice. While the fighting lasts, I can at least grant you the gift of sight so you can see events as they happen.

DHRITARASHTRA: Ah no! I could not bear to see the gushing blood, the mutilated bodies of my loved ones.

Sanjaya enters.

KRISHNA: Then Sanjaya –

STORYTELLER: Sanjaya is King Dhritarashtra's aide.

KRISHNA: I will grant Sanjaya divine sight.
Sanjaya, you will witness all that happens on the field of battle. Whether by day or night, whether openly or in men's hearts. You will narrate it all.

DHRITARASHTRA: Sanjaya, you will be my eyes.

Sanjaya receives the gift of sight.

SANJAYA: My king, they are ready for you.

Dhritarashtra is projected on the screens delivering a state-of-the-nation address announcing the rules of engagement.

DHRITARASHTRA: My fellow countrymen, I address you tonight on the eve of battle, to lay down the rules of combat.
1. The fight will take place between dawn and dusk.
2. No woman will enter the battlefield, and if she does, no warrior will raise weapons against her.
3. Many warriors will not fight a single warrior.
4. No one will interfere when two warriors are locked in a duel.
5. No one will fight an unarmed warrior.

SCENE II: BLESSINGS

A clearing on the battlefield.

BHIMA: Grandfather, we seek your blessings, so that we may fight you as warriors should, and we seek your forgiveness, for we will now see you as our enemy and strike you with our weapons. I do not want to fight you.

BHISHMA: Nor do I, but I am not free, indebted to the Kauravas as I am. I must fight for Duryodhana, and I shall do my best to win for him.
But you may ask a favour of me.

YUDHISHTHIRA: Tell us how our forces can defeat you, you who are known to be invincible. Say, how can you be killed?

BHISHMA: The time for me to die has not yet come. Speak to me at another time.

ARJUNA: Drona, you who taught me how to fight, how can I raise my hand against you?

DRONA: In battle, I am no longer your teacher. You are no longer my student.

YUDHISHTHIRA: How can we defeat you?

DRONA: I will not be defeated unless I quit the fight.

YUDHISHTHIRA: What could make you quit the fight?

DRONA: I would drop my weapon only if a man whose word I trust chooses to lie.

YUDHISHTHIRA: Am I that man?

Conches blare.

BHISHMA: I wish you victory in battle, and good fortune after.

DRONA: I will pray sincerely, every morning, for your victory.

YUDHISHTHIRA: Bhishma Pitamaha, I am suddenly struck by what all this means. I may never clasp you in my arms again. And your voice, an ordinary strand in the fabric of my life, will become a sound bitterly yearned for ... so that, in years to come, a distant voice resembling yours will make me turn my head and weep.

SCENE 12: GATHERING FORCES

Arjuna, Yudhishthira, and Bhima look up and see Duryodhana, like a god, on the screens. He is speaking to an army lining up on the battlefield. Throughout this speech, we get the feeling that millions of people are assembling as armies; people are rallying, getting fired up, turning into animals.

DURYODHANA: The Pandavas have lit a flame that can no longer be extinguished! Krishna says that our land belongs to the Pandavas, that it is theirs by right. By law.

Law? Whose law? Is Krishna king? No. Oh, he's a 'god'? Well, I ask you, what has a god ever done for you?

My friends, I speak truth when I say the Pandavas use Krishna, they hide behind this 'god.'

But let us be clear. We are being robbed in the name of a god. They want to take our land in the name of a god. They want to take our home in the name of a god. They want to make us suffer!

This is an injustice, and we are justice. We rule this land. We are the law. And together, we will protect what's ours. And no one, not Krishna, not the Pandavas, not any man, nor any god, will stand in our way!

A mass of soldiers training for war. The screens reveal a bird's-eye view of the soldiers in movement. As it zooms out, the bodies multiply, revealing millions of people assembling.

STORYTELLER: The armies are assembling. A mass of men and beasts constantly moving, like a river thick with fish. Thousands upon thousands march, confident in battle formations. Both forces are terrible, both beautiful.

The two sides face one another, ten thousand conches blaring out in challenge. The din of cymbals, the deep, heart-stopping throb of war drums.

ACT 7: BHAGAVAD GITA

SCENE 13: THE SONG OF GOD

Arjuna and Krishna stand alone in the middle of the battlefield.

STORYTELLER: Morning breaks on the opening day of war. The rising sun streaks the sky with scarlet, slowly burning off the mist that hangs over the field. The opposing armies, division upon division, stretch as far as the eye follows the curving earth. Arjuna and Krishna ride out into the middle of the field. Armies on both sides. The battlefield, still.

ARJUNA: Krishna, I see no enemies. I see my cousins; my teacher, Drona; my grandfather, Bhishma. I see Duryodhana and his brothers. On the other side, I see my brothers, my sons, nephews, cousins. As if I look in a mirror, we are reflections of each other. In this task of killing family, do I kill myself?
What is justice? What is dharma?
Krishna, my limbs grow weak, my mouth is dry, my body shakes, my hair stands on end. My heart breaks in two – I cannot fight!

KRISHNA: Get to your feet, Arjuna. Behave like the warrior you are.

ARJUNA: A warrior enters battle to preserve dharma. How can it be dharma to strike our kinsmen, to kill those who have nurtured, taught, and grown with us?

KRISHNA: You are confronted by the enormity of the situation, the possibility of failure, the price of success, and you tremble.

ARJUNA: How can I take aim against my elders, who deserve from me my love and reverence? I should be protecting them.
It would be better to give up the kingdom now than gain it at the cost of so much grief. I will not fight!

KRISHNA: Friend, this is unworthy of you.

ARJUNA: Krishna! My thoughts are scattered. My mind is seething like a nest of hornets. I am lost.

STORYTELLER: Then here, with every soldier tense and ready, with every horse straining at its harness; here, in the moment before hell's unleashing, time holds its breath.

Krishna and Arjuna are suspended in time.

Krishna unravels for Arjuna the Mysteries of the Universe.

The Bhagavad Gita is performed as a solo operatic aria. It is a dramatic formal leap in storytelling style, and should help us feel that time is suspended and we are in another realm. The voice of Krishna is sung by an opera singer who is dressed like Krishna. She enters from the left, in a shaft of light, and glides very slowly across the stage. Arjuna and Krishna continue to gesture, also in slow motion, as if they are speaking for a long time. The screens, previously partitioned into multiple sections, now show single enormous images of the cosmos.

VOICE OF KRISHNA:

Verse 1
yadâ yadâ hi dharmasya glânir bhavati bhârata
   I am the changeless and eternal Self, never born, never dying.
abhyutthânam adharmasya tadâtmânaṁ sṛijâmyaham
   I take on material form when humanity is in need
paritrânâya sâdhûnâm vinâshâya cha dushkṛitâm
   To protect the good, to destroy the evil.
dharma-sansthâpanârthâya sambhavâmi yuge yuge
   I shine a light to open your eyes.

Verse 2
mayyâsakta-manâḥ pârtha yogaṁ yuñjan mad-âshrayaḥ
   The world is caught up by appearances.
asanshayam samagram mâm yathâ jñâsyasi tach chhṛinu
   Ego endlessly distracts from seeing the eternal principle
ye chaiva sâttvikâ bhâvâ râjasâs tâmasâûh cha ye
   That the humblest flower
matta eveti tân viddhi na tvaham teshu te mayi
   Is connected to the grandeur of the constellations.

Verse 3
shubhâshubha-phalair evaṁ mokshyase karma-bandhanaiḥ
   Desire and anger cast a screen of smoke over the world.

sannyâsa-yoga-yuktâtmâ vimukto mâm upaiṣhyasi
Make yourself alike in pain and pleasure,
man-manâ bhava mad-bhakto mad-yâjî mâm namaskuru
Profit and loss, victory and defeat,
mâm evaiṣhyasi yuktvaivam âtmânam mat-parâyaṇaḥ
And follow your dharma.

Verse 4
evam jñâtvâ kṛitam karma pûrvair api mumukṣhubhiḥ
Action is the cosmic energy that brings every creature into existence.
kuru karmaiva tasmâttvam pûrvaiḥ pûrvataram kṛitam
Action is inescapable; we always act, even when doing nothing. The question is, how to act rightly?

Verse 5
karmaṇy-evâdhikâras te mâ phaleṣhu kadâchana
Act selflessly, without any thought of personal profit.
mâ karma-phala-hetur bhûr mâ te saṇgo 'stvakarmaṇi
Through selfless service, you will always be fruitful.

Verse 6
tad viddhi praṇipâtena pariprashnena sevayâ
Act without straining after the reward.
upadekṣhyanti te jñânam jñâninas tattva-darshinaḥ
Reward is an illusion.
yaj jñâtvâ na punar moham evam yâsyasi pâṇḍava
Detach action from result,
yena bhûtânyasheṣheṇa drakṣhyasyâtmanyatho mayi
Be my instrument in the battle.

ARJUNA: *(spoken not sung)* How can my purpose be to kill? Is that the true nature of my being?

Verse 7
jâtasya hi dhruvo mṛityur dhruvam janma mṛitasya cha
Arjuna, that which is born will die,
tasmâd aparihârye 'rthe na tvam shochitum arhasi
And that which will die will be reborn. It is pointless to cling and mourn.

ARJUNA: *(spoken not sung)* Krishna, I am overcome by fear. I am confused by what you say.

Who am I? What is my purpose?
My mind is a restless, violent storm.

Verse 8

kârpaṇya-doṣhopahata-svabhâvaḥ
Your mind is creating a veil between you and your dharma.
pṛichchhâmi tvâṁ dharma-sammûḍha-chetâḥ
The fight is not out there, Arjuna, it is inside you.
yach-chhreyaḥ syânnicehchitaṁ brûhi tanme
Fight the emotions inside you, fight the attachment inside you.
shiṣhyaste 'haṁ shâdhi mâṁ tvâṁ prapannam
Control the mind so you can see.

ARJUNA: *(spoken)* Oh Krishna, I long to witness your divinity. Show me your true form.

Krishna reveals his divine manifestation.

I see the entire cosmos turning within your being. If a thousand suns were to rise in the heavens at the same time, the blaze of their light would resemble the splendour of …

Ah! Krishna, your supreme form fills the world, with many gaping mouths and staring eyes, with countless ornaments more beautiful than any seen on Earth. I see you stretched between sky and Earth, Lord. I am like a speck of dust before you, Lord!

Verse 9

kâlo 'smi loka-kṣhaya-kṛit pravṛiddho
I AM TIME, DESTROYER OF WORLDS.
lokân samâhartum iha pravṛittaḥ
I have come to consume the world.
ṛite 'pi tvâṁ na bhaviṣhyanti sarve
Dharma will prevail.
ye 'vasthitâḥ pratyanîkeṣhu yodhâḥ
Rise up, hero. Be my instrument!

აჩ

INTERMISSION

ACT 8: WAR

SCENE 14: BLOODBATH

The curtain is still down. We hear the following:

DHRITARASHTRA: Sanjaya, several times in dreams of this battle I have seen a shining figure, gliding, lance in hand, whose feet do not touch the ground.

SANJAYA: It is Lord Shiva you have seen, lord of the universe, the deathless deity of many names.

DHRITARASHTRA: Sanjaya, what do you see?

SANJAYA: Time unlocks.

The curtain rises and we see several groups clustered around the ruined circle of dirt, now the battlefield of Kurukshetra, bathed in eerie red light. The screens show gathering and dispersing clouds. Sanjaya, between Dhritarashtra and Gandhari, speaks in the centre at the back. At the back left sit the Kauravas, transfixed on the battlefield; at the back right, the Pandavas sit, also watching intently. The Storyteller and a chorus sit on a carpet at the front left, often clapping the talam (rhythm) and voicing solkattu.

Shiva, at the centre, performs a dance of death and destruction. It is haunting, and the music is discordant. Shiva continues to dance throughout the battle as well as narrate the events of the war through Kathakali. He alternates between translating the text of the characters who are speaking, providing another perspective to that which is being voiced, and narrating in Shiva's voice.

The armies clash. Dense showers of arrows fly above them. They hurl themselves at each other. Limbs and carcasses litter the field as far as the eye can see. Heads lie crushed into the mud. The Earth, covered with blood, drinks deep.

Brother hacks at brother, father hacks at son. Comrade blindly swings his sword at comrade. The very planets are engorged with blood and fly amok out of their natural paths. I see meteors falling on our armies and vultures circling the city, a foul disease raking the population. Nature is out of joint!

SCENE 15: FALL OF BHISHMA

In the midst of battle, Yudhishthira speaks to Bhishma.

YUDHISHTHIRA: Pitamaha, you are unbeatable, your skill brings devastation to our troops. What do we do?

BHISHMA: Yudhishthira, while I am alive, you cannot obtain victory.

YUDHISHTHIRA: Must you die for the war to end?

BHISHMA: Do you see another way?

YUDHISHTHIRA: How can you be killed?

BHISHMA: Are you asking me to die?

YUDHISHTHIRA: I am asking you to end all this suffering. The massacre will continue until no life remains.

Battle continues. Interrupted by –

DURYODHANA: Bhishma, our forces shrink, our weapons are dwindling – is our army being strongly led?

BHISHMA: Duryodhana, I have told you many times, the Pandavas will be difficult to overcome.

DURYODHANA: You and Drona are allowing my army to be slaughtered!

BHISHMA: I made you a promise that every day I would kill ten thousand enemy soldiers, and I have done so.

DURYODHANA: But the Pandavas live! You know Arjuna must be defeated, but you hold back.
    If you won't do what it takes to end this war, withdraw from the battle and let Karna fight instead.

Scenes overlap.

YUDHISHTHIRA: If you do not yield, then I will accept defeat.

BHISHMA: NO.

Amba/Shikhandi is seen moving toward Bhishma slowly.

There is a warrior in your army, Shikhandi. I will not fight him. Let him come to me on the battlefield.

In the palace.

SANJAYA: Shikhandi approaches Bhishma. His hands are shaking.

DHRITARASHTRA: Why hasn't Bhishma already killed him?

SANJAYA: Bhishma doesn't move.

BHISHMA: I will not fight a woman.

DHRITARASHTRA: What is she doing on the battlefield?

SANJAYA: There is no woman … It is only Bhishma who sees one. Shikhandi, son of Drupada, moves toward Bhishma, with Arjuna and Krishna behind him.

KRISHNA: Arjuna, you must shoot an arrow quickly.

DHRITARASHTRA: Stop! Stop the battle at once!

SANJAYA: They cannot hear you.

KRISHNA: Arjuna – now!

Arjuna shoots his arrow. Bhishma is struck.

SANJAYA: All stand motionless, some weep, some faint.
     Bhishma's entire body is hidden, arrows sticking out at every angle, his chariot, awash with blood.

ARJUNA: Krishna, how could I strike down this man who nurtured me, who was so dear to me?

KRISHNA: All these events are preordained. Bhishma himself knows this.

ARJUNA: But he was following the rules.

KRISHNA: Why do you assume rules are good?

ARJUNA: He said he saw a woman, he laid down his arms. It was not fair.

KRISHNA: Fairness is a matter of opinion.

ARJUNA: Krishna, surely this cannot be dharma?

KRISHNA: Dharma is a mysterious burden. Who can say what is right and wrong?

Bhishma, struck down, speaks to Duryodhana on the battlefield.

BHISHMA: Duryodhana, my son, I beg you: make peace with the Pandavas, divide this prosperous kingdom as before. Too many brave warriors have already died; think now of the thousands upon thousands who still could return home. Do not let them sleep their final sleep here in the choking mud of Kurukshetra.

DURYODHANA: Grandfather, how were you defeated?
Karna, join the battlefield. Drona will now lead our army. We resume fighting tomorrow at sunrise.

Duryodhana leaves. Bhishma and Karna are alone.

BHISHMA: Go fight your senseless battle. Karna, come to me, my young rival.

KARNA: Why, Bhishma? You have always looked upon me with hate.

BHISHMA: I know who you are – I know you are Kunti's son. End this war, join the Pandavas.

KARNA: Give me your blessing now to enter the battlefield.

BHISHMA: Go then. Tell the king I am still alive. I will lie here on my bed of arrows until the sun rises each day closer to the pole star. Then I will release my final breath. For now, face me toward the west. I want to see your father.

Dhritarashtra in the palace.

DHRITARASHTRA: Ah! Bhishma the Invincible has fallen? My heart must be made of adamantine stone that it hasn't shattered at this dreadful news.
Oh Bhishma, you are like a god in strength and skill. If you have fallen, then what hope is there for my sons?

SCENE 16: THE DEATH OF ABHIMANYU

STORYTELLER: Day 13. Abhimanyu, son of Arjuna, was only fifteen years old. Though instructed by his father to stay home, Abhimanyu was eager to join the battle.

DRONA: Chakravyuha!

Shiva dances the story as Sanjaya tells it. At times, he takes on the character of Abhimanyu and the other soldiers in this scene.

SANJAYA: Drona puts in place a battle formation so intricately designed that no man can escape: ten thousand of Drona's men into wheel formation, rotating, winding, circular, impossible to penetrate – ten thousand trained, courageous warriors, advancing as one, a sight to strike fear in all who witness it.

YUDHISHTHIRA: Abhimanyu, son of Arjuna, you are still a boy, but in courage and skill you rival your great father. You are the only one who knows how to break into the wheel. Child, for the sake of all of us, you must penetrate what Drona has constructed.

STORYTELLER AS ABHIMANYU: Uncle, I know how to enter the wheel, but not how to come out again.

YUDHISHTHIRA: Once you have broken in, you will force a path for us to follow. We will be close behind and smash it open from within.

STORYTELLER AS ABHIMANYU: Today, the world will witness my great feats; I shall slaughter all who challenge me or I'll not call myself Arjuna's son!

SANJAYA: He flies like a mad moth into a searing fire!
   The boy brings chaos to his adversaries, Kaurava heads rolling on the ground. Slicing off hands, arms, ears, so that the ground is an altar sluiced with sacrificial blood.
   Yudhishthira and Bhima cannot penetrate the wheel.
   So the young prince stands surrounded by uncles, teachers, grandfathers, alone, unprotected.

Wave after wave of warriors rush at him; one by one, his weapons are destroyed, his bow broken, his spear splintered, his chariot smashed. Now he fights on foot, nothing left to defend himself.

A mace smashes the young hero's head.

Abhimanyu, Arjuna's best beloved, beautiful in death as he was in life, falls to earth and does not move again. It is as though the moon has fallen from the sky to the black earth.

At the palace.

GANDHARI: These were great warriors; they knew full well that a mob attack on a lone opponent was contrary to dharma – yet they did it.

DHRITARASHTRA: I wish we had made peace with the Pandavas. If only we had taken heed when Krishna came as their envoy. But Duryodhana was foolish, and this devastation is the result. Are we reduced to killing children now? Oh god, we have become animals.

SANJAYA: You should blame yourself; you had a hundred chances to guide your son with a restraining hand. You pandered to his greed – your lamentations are like the hollow clank of empty vessels, and come too late.

On the battlefield.

ARJUNA: Krishna, you knew this would happen?

KRISHNA: Yes.

ARJUNA: Is that why you kept me away?

KRISHNA: Yes.

ARJUNA: My son is dead. You let my son die.

KRISHNA: Remember what I told you. Beings have mysterious origins. They emerge into light, then disappear into shadow. Recognize all this is illusion.

ARJUNA: Oh, my little boy, my arms ache to hold you. I long for the smell of your skin, your hair, oh I am hungry for the sight of you. If I never see your face again, how can I live?

Transition to a new scene, as Shiva dances.

STORYTELLER: Arjuna avenges Abhimanyu's murder, setting off the next spree of killing. All rules are lost, time moves relentlessly, marked by the sun indifferently sailing through the heavens.

They begin to fight at night; warriors soar through the darkness, torches light their way as they call out names, blind to who is friend and who is foe. It is as if the stars themselves have descended to the earth, colliding in a cosmic battle. The Earth drinks deep.

SCENE 17: DEATH OF DRONA

KRISHNA: Drona's onslaught annihilates our army. He must be removed from the battle.

BHIMA: How can Drona be removed?

KRISHNA: He lives for his son Ashwatthama. If his son were dead, he would lose his resolve.

YUDHISHTHIRA: But Ashwatthama is a powerful warrior. It will take us days to defeat him.

KRISHNA: We don't want to defeat Ashwatthama. We want Drona to quit the fight. You must tell him his son is dead.

YUDHISHTHIRA: Krishna, that would be a lie.

BHIMA: I have an idea.

He leaves.

KRISHNA: From where does your desire to tell the truth come? To look good or to do good?

YUDHISHTHIRA: Why are we fighting if not to preserve the truth?

KRISHNA: Is truth so important?

Bhima returns.

BHIMA: There. I have killed an elephant and named it Ashwatthama. Now Ashwatthama is dead.

Yudhishthira hesitates.

KRISHNA: What if a lie could end the war?

BHIMA: DRONA! I have killed Ashwatthama. Ashwatthama is dead.

DRONA: Ashwatthama is too skilled a warrior. I don't believe you. Yudhishthira, is what Bhima says true?

KRISHNA: *(to Yudhishthira)* To speak untruth in order to save lives is not a sin.

YUDHISHTHIRA: Yes. It is true. Bhima has killed Ashwatthama. Ashwatthama is dead.

STORYTELLER: Drona lays down his bow and other weapons and composes himself in meditation.
    Dhrishtadyumna, brother of Draupadi, grabs Drona by the hair, raises his sword, and cuts off his head, raising it high in triumph.

All fall to their knees.

DURYODHANA: Oh, Krishna, why do you help the Pandavas?

KRISHNA: Reflect on all the wrongs the Pandavas have suffered at your unrighteous hands, Duryodhana. Just think about the death of Abhimanyu. On this side of the balance there is Bhishma and, yes, Drona.
    But sinfulness cannot always be countered by narrow virtue. Ends justify means.

DURYODHANA: Karna, tomorrow you will lead our armies. Kill Arjuna, make the Pandavas pay!

KARNA: Brother, tomorrow Arjuna will die, and I will give you victory over all the world, or I will die in the attempt.

SCENE 18: KUNTI AND KARNA

The screens descend and create a backdrop to the scene. It is morning. Only Kunti and Karna are onstage.

STORYTELLER: Day 17. Sunlight falls on Karna's radiant face as he stands deep in prayer, as every morning. Now that he knows who his true father is, Karna worships him with even more devotion. Kunti descends to the battlefield to meet with father and son. Trembling, she approaches Karna.

KUNTI: Karna.

KARNA: The charioteer's son salutes the mother of the Pandavas.

KUNTI: Forgive me.

KARNA: Your voice pierces my ears as if a voice from a previous birth and stirs strange pain.

KUNTI: In the first dawn of your life, it was I who introduced you to this wide world.

KARNA: Why are you here alone? This is a battlefield, and I am commander of the Kaurava army.

KUNTI: Child, I have come to beg a favour of you.

KARNA: A boon? That's what you want? You came here not to give love to your outcast first-born, but to collect charity from the charioteer's son.

KUNTI: I do not want brother to fight brother. Abandon the Kauravas, take your rightful place among your family. Let there be peace.

KARNA: Peace for whom? Them or me?

KUNTI: I do not want my sons to die.

KARNA: Who do you refer to? The ones born after marriage or the one born before?

KUNTI: I speak for you all. All of my sons, especially you, my first-born.

KARNA: How often in the depth of night I have had this very dream, that slowly, softly, my mother would come to see me, just like this.
    Oh, royal mother, loving woman, be this real or dream, on the eve of battle, your voice fills me so much that my heart rushes toward the five Pandavas, calling them brothers!

KUNTI: Then come, son, come with me.

KARNA: Yes, Mother, I will go with you. I won't ask questions. Without a doubt or worry, I will go. Lady, you are my mother! And your call has awakened my soul. No longer can I hear the drums of battle or victory's conch shells. Lady, one more time, say I am your son.

KUNTI: Karna, you are my son!

KARNA: Then why did you discard me so ingloriously to the mercy of this blind unknown world? Why did you let me float away on the current of contempt so irreversibly?

KUNTI: Child, let your reprimands like a hundred thunderclaps rend this heart of mine into a thousand pieces.

KARNA: All these years, you have witnessed me slighted and abused within the court. And you've said nothing.

KUNTI: That I cast you aside is a curse that haunts me.

KARNA: The world knows you as the mother of five sons. At the end of this war, I promise you that you will still have five sons, including one great archer. Either Arjuna or me.

KUNTI: Please –

KARNA: I can see the end, full of peace and emptiness. The side that is going to lose – Please don't ask me to desert that side. Let Pandu's children win and become kings, let me stay with the losers, those whose hopes will be dashed.

KUNTI: Is there nothing I can say to change your mind? To bring you peace?

KARNA: The night of my birth, you left me upon the earth, nameless, homeless. In the same way today, Mother, be ruthless and just abandon me.

Kunti leaves. Karna prepares to die.

SCENE 19: DEATH OF KARNA

STORYTELLER: The hour of Karna's death is fast approaching. Time itself, whispering in his ear …

The screen and ropes are all raised to the sky, revealing the entire, wide-open space of the empty stage.

KARNA: Who has caught hold of my wheel? What trick is this, Krishna?

KRISHNA: The Earth herself has you in her claws, Karna. It is she who devours your chariot wheel, not me.

KARNA: Hold off, Arjuna! Only a coward strikes when his opponent has laid down his arms.

KRISHNA: Arjuna, don't let up now! Kill him while you can –

KARNA: Arjuna, you observe dharma; do what you know is right!

KRISHNA: It is well and good for you to plead dharma when you're in trouble. But where has dharma been while you have stood by the unrighteous Duryodhana?

DURYODHANA: Karna, call your greatest weapon.

KARNA: Yes, I know the secret mantra.

KRISHNA: *(to Arjuna)* What is holding you back? Strike!

DURYODHANA: Karna! Speak the words!

KARNA: I call upon … I call …

He struggles to recall the words of the mantra that Parashurama taught him, but his mind is blurred; he cannot remember them.

KRISHNA: Arjuna, take his life.

Arjuna shoots. Karna is pierced and immediately killed.

SANJAYA: Karna falls, the rivers cease to flow, the sun turns pale, the Earth trembles.

Duryodhana mourns Karna.

SCENE 20: DEATH OF DURYODHANA

GANDHARI *(calling out to Duryodhana from the palace)* Duryodhana, my son, I beg you, stop this madness.

BHIMA: DURYODHANA!

DURYODHANA: BHIMA!

Bhima arrives with a large wooden mace.

DURYODHANA: I am not afraid of you, wolf-belly!

BHIMA: I have waited thirteen years for this!
I took pleasure in crushing every one of your ninety-nine brother's skulls with my bare hands. And now I will avenge Draupadi for what you did to her.
Today I shall regain our kingdom!

They fight with maces first. Then, when the weapons are lost, they wrestle to exhaustion. Nobody is winning. Duryodhana is more skilled but Bhima is stronger.

KRISHNA: *(to Bhima)* Hit him low – in the legs. He is vulnerable there.

YUDHISHTHIRA: Strike his thigh!

Krishna slaps his own thigh. Bhima sees the sign. Seizing his chance, he smashes his mace full strength against Duryodhana's thigh, breaking it instantly.

DURYODHANA: AH! Shame on you, Bhima!
Krishna, you cheated! The rules were clear: no blow must strike below the belt. Krishna, because of your devious and sinful ways, the Pandavas, who should have lost this war, have won.

KRISHNA: Son of Gandhari, it is the Earth herself that has won. This bloody field of Kurukshetra is due to you alone – you would not hear the wisdom of your elders.

DURYODHANA: I have lived a good life in my kingdom.
Bhima, you and your brothers have spent your life in the forest like beggars and thieves, and now you inherit a world of corpses. Today, I die a warrior on the battlefield. The Earth is a widow – you can take her.

Blackout.

ACT 9: HUMANS

SCENE 21: AFTERMATH

Three funeral pyres are lit. The rest of the play has very little light – the funeral pyres light the scene.

STORYTELLER: The war is over.

The field is a monument to death – the ground a mess of bones and hair and hides, skulls gathered in heaps waiting to be dealt with. The remains of funeral pyres everywhere.

Over one billion people were killed in this war. The bodies are burned, the ashes are released into the river Ganga.

The Pandavas rejoice, boasting and arguing about who was the greatest warrior in battle. There was a spectator of the war, who stood perched high up on a mountain overlooking the field, so they asked him, who was the greatest warrior? Was it Arjuna? Bhima? Duryodhana? But he just looked at them, confused. He said he did not see Arjuna fight Karna, he did not see Bhima kill Duryodhana … He only saw Shiva's feet, dancing furiously and destroying all the unrighteous kings in order to save the Earth.

SCENE 22: RAGE OF ELDERS

GANDHARI: Krishna, who am I now? I am Gandhari, childless mother of one hundred sons. Is there no word for women such as I, a word like 'widow,' another word for 'empty'?

DHRITARASHTRA: Duryodhana! Oh, my tragic son. Oh, the Earth has stolen him! The Earth has triumphed over all of us.

GANDHARI: I curse you, Krishna, for presiding over this tragic conflict! In thirty-six years' time, your family will suffer the same fate as us. They will tear themselves apart and your own womenfolk will weep as inconsolably as we do now.

KRISHNA: Don't give way to anguish; grief breeds grief. You're wise enough to know that. You, yourself, are by no means blameless.

DHRITARASHTRA: Unfeeling man, how can we not grieve?
Oh, my son! How can a kingdom, however rich, be worth your life, oh, my precious son.

STORYTELLER: The Pandavas go to pay their respects to their aunt and uncle. /They come to beg for their forgiveness.

YUDHISHTHIRA: /I come to beg for your forgiveness. I am the killer of your sons, I have caused devastation upon this Earth ... I am not fit to govern.

GANDHARI: Come now, it is we who should be crushed by grief. Have we not lost a hundred sons, as if they were never born? You have gained all that you were fighting for. Shame! Oh, shame on you, Yudhishthira!

DHRITARASHTRA: How can a king claiming to know dharma kill his kin so cruelly? How will you rule without your grandfather and your teachers around you?

GANDHARI: Oh, Bhima, could you not have spared us just one son, one who would live to comfort us in our old age?

DHRITARASHTRA: I hope you are happy with your victory, your capture of the Earth. I hope you enjoy her after the slaughter of our shining sons.

SCENE 23: BED OF ARROWS

STORYTELLER: In the days following the war, Bhishma lies on his bed of arrows. Yudhishthira watches the living rush onto the battlefield searching for the bodies of their loved ones, looking for a face, a ring, an amulet, anything to distinguish them from the others ...

YUDHISHTHIRA: What have we done?

BHISHMA: Son of Pandu, why are you not rejoicing? You have won this Earth and won it righteously.

YUDHISHTHIRA: Why then does victory taste as bitter as defeat?

BHISHMA: My grandson, now that the war is won, you must turn to the battle for your mind.

YUDHISHTHIRA: I can't stay here. I am going to renounce everything and live in the forest.

BHISHMA: You can renounce the world, become a hermit, but what about your kingdom?

YUDHISHTHIRA: I want only peace, Grandfather.

BHISHMA: A hermit seeks peace for himself, but only a king can create a world where peace is possible for everyone. Choose kingship, Yudhishthira.

YUDHISHTHIRA: Why me?

BHISHMA: Who better than you?

YUDHISHTHIRA: When I had the crown, I gambled away my kingdom.

BHISHMA: So you can empathize with your subjects' imperfections. You, who silently suffered thirteen years of exile, know the power of repentance and forgiveness. You, who saw Duryodhana reject every offer of peace, know the power of the ego and the horror of adharma. You, who had to lie to kill your own teacher, know the complexities of dharma. Only you, son of Kunti, have the power to establish a world where the head is balanced with the heart. Your rule will be for the future generations.

YUDHISHTHIRA: What future? All our sons are murdered! And you who speak of future generations? You gave up your throne for your own father's happiness.

BHISHMA: And what has come of that but pain and death? Be the Dharma King, Yudhishthira. Restore the Kingdom.

STORYTELLER: Bhishma and Yudhishthira spoke for hours. Yudhishthira would ask him a question, and Bhishma would respond with a story. He told Yudhishthira hundreds of stories over this time.

BHISHMA: Krishna, my time has come.

KRISHNA: If you can hear me, Bhishma, I want you to know that I am here and so are all your kin.

BHISHMA: So many days have passed while I have lain here, it seems a century.

Dhritarashtra, I want you to stop grieving for your sons. What has happened was preordained long ago and could not have been other than it was. Treat the Pandavas as your own sons, they will protect you.

Bhishma chants the thousand names of god. The earth shifts its axis, and Bhishma releases his life.

SCENE 24: RETREAT OF ELDERS

DHRITARASHTRA: I find no peace thinking of the horrors of the war fought for my sake.

Gandhari, come, let's retreat to a life in the forest.

STORYTELLER: Dhritarashtra and Gandhari leave. Not far behind them, Kunti follows …

YUDHISHTHIRA: Mother, why are you leaving? How can you abandon us?

KUNTI: Karna …

YUDHISHTHIRA: Mother, why do you weep for the charioteer's son?

KUNTI: He was your brother.

YUDHISHTHIRA: Karna was our brother?

ARJUNA: Why didn't you tell us?

KUNTI: I grieve bitterly for the man who was and was not my son. I wish to go with wise Gandhari and Dhritarashtra.

STORYTELLER: So Kunti also leaves. For years the elders live a humble life in the forest, until one day a fire breaks out nearby. Dhritarashtra is the first to smell the smoke. 'Run,' he says. 'Why?' says Gandhari. 'Why indeed?' says Kunti. So they sit there. And wait for a wall of flames to engulf them.

Krishna stands to exit.

Krishna, you are leaving too?

KRISHNA: Yes, I have played my part in this story. Dharma has been preserved, and it will be restored by Yudhishthira. He will bring peaceful co-existence to the generations to come.

YUDHISHTHIRA: How can I when all our children have been slaughtered in this horrific battle?

KRISHNA: I have spared one life. A child grows in the belly of Uttara.

STORYTELLER: The widow of Abhimanyu. That child, the great-grandson of Arjuna, will grow to rule for future generations until he is killed by a snake named Takshaka.

YUDHISHTHIRA: Krishna, what will happen to you? Where will you go?

KRISHNA: Gandhari's curse will come true, and in thirty-six years' time, my family will destroy themselves in another war. The Earth will swallow the whole kingdom ... The sky will grow black. The sea will retreat from the land, then crash forward, savaging the city with watery claws, devouring streets, squares, palaces, and gardens. The houses of the poor will dissolve instantly. The mansions of the rich will take a little longer. Every one of the buildings, every tower and pinnacle, will be drowned, as if that kingdom, those people, had never been.

YUDHISHTHIRA: How do you live, knowing this will be true?

KRISHNA: We are born; we die. And, in between, we briefly act. We are like transient bubbles arising on the surface of a stream: not here, then here, and then again not here.

STORYTELLER: And just like that, Krishna was gone.

A song of lament. The ensembles leave the downstage stools, walking upstage and forming a line, leaving only the Storyteller and Yudhishthira.

SCENE 25: THE FINAL JOURNEY

STORYTELLER: One final journey.
    Yudhishthira is an old man. He arrives at the gates of heaven and falls at Indra's feet.

YUDHISHTHIRA: I have walked for months in the cold of Mount Himvat, my wife and brothers dying along the way. Releasing myself of attachment has been as bitter as this cold.

For thirty-six years I have ruled as king. People lived in harmony, and greed was kept at bay. Abhimanyu's son grew to be a wise and noble man, like his father, Abhimanyu, and his grandfather, Arjuna. I left the kingdom in his hands. Here I stand, alone. Allow me to enter the gates of heaven.

STORYTELLER: A dog had wandered next to Yudhishthira and followed him for the journey. Indra says, 'You are not alone. Who is this dog by your side?'

YUDHISHTHIRA: He has stayed with me on the long passage.

STORYTELLER AS INDRA: Leave this dog here and come with me to heaven.

YUDHISHTHIRA: Through our entire journey he has walked beside me loyally, sharing all hardships. This dog must come with me.

STORYTELLER AS INDRA: Impossible.

YUDHISHTHIRA: I cannot abandon him. It would be wicked to cast aside this dog who is so devoted to me to fulfill my own selfish desire for the joys of heaven.

STORYTELLER AS INDRA: But you have released all other ties; you left your wife and brothers lying on the ground. Why is this dog different?

YUDHISHTHIRA: They were already dead. There was nothing more that I could do for them. This dog is alive. To abandon him would be equivalent to the worst sins – I cannot, I will not do it.

STORYTELLER: Suddenly the dog transformed; it was the God Dharma – Yudhishthira's father.

'My son, I am so pleased with you. There is no one in all the worlds more virtuous than you. Enter the gates of heaven, Yudhishthira … Open your eyes.' Yudhishthira opens his eyes in heaven, and the first person he sees is …

YUDHISHTHIRA: Duryodhana?

How can this be! This wicked cousin of ours, this man, driven by greed and bitter envy, was responsible for the deaths of millions. Yet here he sits enjoying the rewards of Indra's heaven! I cannot even look at him. Let me go where my brothers are.

STORYTELLER AS INDRA: Heaven knows no enmity. Put the past behind you.

YUDHISHTHIRA: I wish to go to my brothers – Karna, Arjuna, Bhima, Draupadi. Where my loved ones are – that is heaven.

STORYTELLER: So Yudhishthira is guided down the long and dark path to the other realm, where he hears terrible cries in the darkness.

YUDHISHTHIRA: Who are you?

KARNA: I am Karna.

BHIMA: I am Bhima.

ARJUNA: I am Arjuna.

DRAUPADI: I am Draupadi.

YUDHISHTHIRA: What madness is this? What have these beloved people done that they should be consigned to hell like this? It makes no sense that Duryodhana should enjoy every luxury while my family suffers like this! Am I dreaming? Is this a delusion?

STORYTELLER AS INDRA: Yudhishthira, you have released your kingdom, your wealth, your clothes. But you have not released your anger.
 Thirty-six years ago, you killed the Kauravas. You won their kingdom and have ruled it, and still you have not forgiven them? In life Duryodhana clung to his kingdom, and in death you cling to your hate. How then can you hope to attain peace in heaven?
 This realization humbles Yudhishthira. He falls to his knees and weeps.

SCENE 26: JAYA

The storyteller sits on a stool, the entire ensemble in the shadows standing in a line behind her.

STORYTELLER: The storyteller concludes the narration. Snakes still hang suspended in the air over the sacrificial fire, priests still stand at the altar impatient to conclude their ritual. By now, the blazing fire has reduced to a flame. All eyes are on King Janamejaya, who looks confused.

'Who is the hero of this story? Who is the villain?'

'My king, I told you not to be confused by the plots and characters. The story is an illusion for you to receive a deeper meaning.'

'This is the history of my ancestors, it's the story of their great victory in a battle.'

'Yes, my king, that's true. The Pandavas were victorious on the battlefield of Kurukshetra, but in heaven, when Yudhishthira released his anger, he achieved an even greater victory, victory over himself. That spiritual victory is what your ancestors want you to inherit.'

Janamejaya begins to weep. 'I miss my father.'

'I know.'

'I want revenge.'

'I know. Takshaka killed your father for justice. You kill the snakes for justice. More orphans will yearn for that same justice.'

The king asks, 'Who decides what justice is?'

The storyteller is silent.

Janamejaya shouts, 'This story brings no comfort. No peace.'

'But the wisdom contained within it can, my king.'

Janamejaya looks up into the eyes of one of the snakes hanging above him ... In her eyes he sees his own anger, his rage, his fear.

And the lotus of wisdom blooms in Janamejaya's mind.

'You are right, this sacrifice is not dharma. Stop the burning; no more snakes will be killed.'

The entire kingdom exhales as King Janamejaya closes his eyes.

Om. Shanti, Shanti, Shanti.

Om. Peace, peace, peace.

Blackout.

WHY NOT THEATRE'S *MAHABHARATA*: SOURCES AND INFLUENCES

By Karen Fricker and Lawrence Switzky

Karen Fricker and Lawrence Switzky have followed the creation of Why Not Theatre's Mahabharata *since 2018. Karen Fricker is a Toronto-based theatre critic and academic. Lawrence Switzky is Associate Professor of English and Drama at the University of Toronto.*

Mahabharata is a story about the telling of a story. Or, rather, it's many stories about the telling of many stories. Tradition attributes authorship, in different ways, to the sage Vyasa. Some accounts have the elephant-headed god Ganesha ordering Vyasa to speak the *Mahabharata* story to him without interruption so that Ganesha can write it down (Hawley and Pillai 2021, 4). Theatre scholar M. L. Varadpande also attributes composition of the story to Vyasa but has him first narrating the epic to his son Shuka (11). Accounts generally agree that Vyasa wrote himself into the story as the grandfather of the main figures of the story, the Pandava and Kaurava cousins.

Already it's clear that to approach *Mahabharata* is to contend with a deep and not-always-straightforward history of storytelling and meta-storytelling, with subsequent generations taking on the stories and crafting their own versions. As scholars Nell Shapiro Hawley and Sohini Sarah Pillai put it, '[f]or the last two thousand years, the most common response to the *Mahabharata* has been to recreate it' (2021, 3). They also note that for most people growing up in the South Asian diaspora, the written Sanskrit epic is not their first encounter with *Mahabharata*. These stories have always been told across a variety of media, in a culture that is continuously alive with oral, visual, and theatrical instances: 'When you read or hear or see one *Mahabharata*, you are aware of others in the background. You're naturally experiencing it in a comparative way. You can hear what's not there, in addition to what is' (2023).

Mahabharata has been retold as verbal storytelling, in song, in dance, in performance, and through many forms of writing, including novels, poetry, historical epics, and more. India-born British scholar and journalist

Chindu Sreedharan even brought the stories to social media in a series of 2,700 tweets from 2009 to 2013. As they created their version, Miriam Fernandes and Ravi Jain drew directly on Carole Satyamurti's poetic version of *Mahabharata* as well as on many previous tellings and commentaries.

We focus in this essay on some of these retellings that were a particular influence on Why Not Theatre's production, including family oral traditions; popular-culture versions, including TV series and comic books; and the best-known stage version in the West, Peter Brook's production of Jean-Claude Carrière's script, which sparked an important dialogue about cultural appropriation after it toured the world in the late 1980s.

Jain's first exposure to the epic was through oral and pop-culture adaptations. As a Canadian-born son of parents born in India, '*Mahabharata* was a story that played in the background of my childhood,' he says. The *Khana and Kahani* portion of this production pays homage to childhood experiences. 'It's really rare for someone to hear the story from beginning to end,' says Jain. 'Normally the way people receive the story is over a meal, and an elder will tell you not just one story but the meaning within the story.' *Khana and Kahani* is a scripted conversation between Sharada K Eswar and either Fernandes or Jain about an episode involving a nature spirit that is not otherwise told in the show.

Another significant influence on Jain was the Hindi-language TV series created by B. R. Chopra, which premiered on Indian television in 1988 and British television in 1991. Over ninety-four episodes, Chopra's encyclopedic *Mahabharat* relayed the rivalry of the Pandavas and the Kauravas as a lavish costume drama with occasionally janky special effects; the battle at Kurukshetra featured more than 15,000 extras. Each new episode, announced with the now-famous theme song 'Ath Shri Mahabharat Katha,' emptied the streets as viewers flocked inside to watch it. Jain and many members of the cast recall Chopra's series playing at a relative's house or gathering around a VHS or DVD player on the weekend for family viewing.

Jain and Fernandes consulted filmic tellings of *Ramayana* and *Mahabharata* as well, particularly cartoons. One point of reference was Nina Paley's *Sita Sings the Blues* (2008), which sets the ancient story of the devoted and then exiled wife of Prince Rama alongside the modern-day account of a cartoonist in San Francisco who is abandoned by her husband, and combines Indian shadow puppets, animated eighteenth-century Rajput paintings, and sketches from the artist's notebook. Another was *Arjun: The Warrior Prince* (2012), co-produced by UTV Motion Pictures and Walt Disney Pictures, which follows Arjuna's coming-of-age, and, like Why Not's *Mahabharata*, is narrated in flashback by a storyteller – in this case, by a maid to a young prince in Viratnagar, where the Pandavas are hiding in disguise. *Arjun* likewise blends multiple influences and traditions, including the rotoscoping of classical Disney animated features, Japanese manga and anime, and digital effects, to tell an action-packed classical Indian story.

Another vital, influential genre of *Mahabharata* retellings are comic books and graphic novels, most famously the Amar Chitra Katha ('Immortal Picture Stories') comic book series published by Mumbai-based Indian Book House. Founded in 1967 to publish classic Indian stories in the English language, Amar Chitra Katha started publishing stories from *Mahabharata* in 1970 with titles such as 'The Pandava Princes' and 'The Gita.' In 1985 it announced an ambitious plan to release a sixty-issue series that would tell the entire 'immortal epic of Vyasa' (quoted in Pritchett 85) but this was eventually truncated to forty-two issues. As Francis W. Pritchett has documented, the founder of Amar Chitra Katha, Anant Pai, was enterprising in his distribution methods, initially giving free copies to schools, many of which subscribed once they realized the comic books' educational effectiveness. Individuals and families could also buy annual subscriptions.

Members of the Why Not team attest personally to the pervasive popularity and influence of these comic-book retellings. Being Catholics from Goa, Miriam Fernandes's family does not have a strong faith-based attachment to *Mahabharata*, but her parents nonetheless grew up reading the Amar Chitra Katha series in the 1970s. Composer Suba Sankaran had a personal connection to Amar Chitra Katha – her uncle used to write and illustrate for the company – and recalls reading the *Mahabharata* titles on family visits to India. She continues to collect them today.

Material from *Mahabharata* has continued to appear in what is now called graphic novel form: Hawley and Pillai note the publication of no fewer than four English-language graphic novels telling parts of the *Mahabharata* stories between 2012 and 2017 (28). A particularly noteworthy further appearance of *Mahabharata* content in graphic novel form was a trilogy published in 2014–15 by Campfire Graphic Novels in India and marketed in the United States by Random House. As Philip Lutgendorf argues, *The Kaurava Empire* shows the clear influence of George Lucas's *Star Wars* universe in its reimagining 'of the *Mahabharata* war in the setting of an intergalactic empire during an unspecified future eon' (371). While science fiction was not popular on the Indian subcontinent prior to the late twentieth century, Lutgendorf argues that *Star Wars* – with its setting in a slightly dilapidated future and its narrative roots in mytho-poetic struggles between heroes and the 'dark side' – had particular resonances with Indian culture emerging into 'technological and consumer possibility' at the turn of the twenty-first century (368).

The first stage version of *Mahabharata* to have an impact on Ravi Jain was Peter Brook's influential, controversial production that toured the world in the late 1980s. As he discusses in an interview with Fernandes in this volume, he saw the filmed version of Brook's *Mahabharata* in approximately 2001 and was struck by how the material felt at once familiar and unfamiliar to him as someone who'd grown up with popular-culture and familial tellings of parts of the *Mahabharata* but no broader knowledge of *Mahabharata* traditions.

Brook's *Mahabharata* was indeed a landmark event raising awareness in Western cultural circles about the epic. It also became a fierce point of debate in what theatre scholar Ric Knowles dubbed the 'interculture wars' (21) of the late twentieth and early twenty-first centuries. The work of Brook's Centre international de créations théâtrales in Paris focused from the late 1970s on staging a *Mahabharata*, which premiered at the 1985 Avignon Festival as a twelve–hour cycle of three plays (Williams 19). After an extensive research period with Brook, Jean-Claude Carrière took three years to write a final draft of the script, and the rehearsal period, which included a trip to India for everyone involved, was six months long (21). The production's three parts – 'The Game of Dice,' 'The Exile in the Forest,' and 'The War' – presented, in theatre scholar David Williams's words, 'a mythic journey from disruption to reintegration [...] a morality play or cautionary tale alarmingly pertinent to a divided post-nuclear world' (22).

The company featured actors from nineteen nations, only one of whom, Mallika Sarabhai, who played Draupadi, was from India (Bharucha 1642). The production then moved to the Bouffes du Nord in Paris, the home of Brook's Centre international, and then toured in 1987–89 to six countries on four continents (Williams 21). In each location, Brook rejected conventional and existing venues in favour of locations that had 'a palpable quality of weathered textured humanity' (ibid.), including rock quarries in Avignon, Athens, Perth, and Adelaide, and the previously abandoned Majestic Theatre in Brooklyn. When the production played at the Majestic, 'it was considered the major event of the New York season [...] virtually every ticket was sold' (Carlson 49).

A significant critique emerged of Brook's *Mahabharata*, arguing that he was not doing justice to the material by removing it from its specific context within Hindu culture and history. In a 1987 article, India-born scholar and critic Gautam Dasgupta argued that Brook's production rendered *Mahabharata* 'an empty shell' because the stories and actions in it were not tied back to 'a deeply-ingrained structure of ritual beliefs and ethical codes of conduct' (11) that would be familiar to Indian audiences. Brook and Carrière were reading the material through a Western lens, argued Dasgupta, using the *Iliad* and *Odyssey* as their paradigms for epic storytelling and writing the material in ways that resonated 'with Shakespearean themes' (13). They made Krishna a Prospero figure and Kunti, Gandhari, and Draupudi echoes of King Lear's daughters.

Indian theatre artist and scholar Rustom Bharucha extended this line of argument in a stinging essay published in 1988 in *Economic and Political Weekly* and subsequently republished in numerous other outlets. Bharucha classed Brook's production as 'one of the most blatant (and accomplished) appropriations of Indian culture in recent years' (1642), making direct links between what he characterized as Brook's cultural plundering and British colonization of India. Bharucha critiqued the ways in which Brook and Carrière's storytelling did not reflect the circular nature of time in the source material – 'Nothing could be more foreign to the *Mahabharata* than linearity' (1644) – and the use of the character of a boy as the passive listener to Vyasa's storytelling, which 'disarms criticism and compels us to watch the play with naive wonder' (ibid.).

Brook did not deny that he had downplayed the Indian elements of the *Mahabharata*, rather arguing that 'he had found in this great epic a global voice, accessible to all humanity' (Carlson 53). Bharucha set the terms of intercultural debates in the performing arts for many years to come by arguing against the premise that 'the *Mahabharata* is Indian but it is universal.' Countered Bharucha, the *Mahabharata* 'is universal *because* it is Indian. One cannot separate the culture from the text' (1634).

Acknowledging the contentious nature of Brook's production, Jain also notes the influence of Brook's directing style on his own. In *Mahabharata* and other Brook productions, Jain was impressed by the powerful simplicity and minimalism of Brook's stage storytelling and recognizes that he borrows from that style in his work. Rustom Bharucha has also been involved in Why Not Theatre's *Mahabharata*: he reached out to the company during the COVID-19 pandemic, and Fernandes and Jain sent him their script, leading to a number of lengthy conversations that helped them refocus their storytelling on the three main themes of dharma, storytelling, and ecocide. While Bharucha did not play an official role in the production as a dramaturg or advisor, 'chatting with him always sparks new things,' says Fernandes. 'He always takes us somewhere that we didn't expect to go and opens up other doors to explore.'

Why Not's *Mahabharata* is a compression of a narrative cosmos, though it is infused with dozens of other tellings – from across time and around the world. Hawley and Pillai remind us, in fact, not to try to tell the complete story of *Mahabharata*, unless we wish to invoke the 'long-standing curse that is said to befall those who take on the epic as a whole' (2021, 15). Not risking the curse, Fernandes, Jain, and their collaborators have crafted their *Mahabharata* out of a selection of the stories and previous tellings that most resonate with them as Canada-based theatre artists from the South Asian diaspora, taking their place in a tradition that will extend forward in ways that we cannot yet imagine. Why Not's *Mahabharata* concludes with the lotus of wisdom blooming in the mind of King Janamejaya, who has been listening to the Storyteller. It's also an invitation for audiences to take their own insights and to tell the story again, from their traditions and perspectives.

Works Cited

Bharucha, Rustom. 'Peter Brook's "Mahabharata": A View from India.' *Economic and Political Weekly*, vol. 23, no. 32, 1988, pp. 1642–47.

Carlson, Marvin. 'Peter Brook's "The Mahabharata" and Ariane Mnouchkine's 'L'Indiade' as Examples of Contemporary Cross-Cultural Theatre.' *The Dramatic Touch of Difference: Theatre, Own and Foreign*, edited by Erika Fischer-Lichte, Josephine Riley, and Michael Gissenwehrer, Gunter Narr Varlag Tubingen, 1990, pp. 49–56.

Dasgupta, Gautam. 'The *Mahabharata*: Peter Brook's "Orientalism".' *Performing Arts Journal*, vol. 10, no. 3, 1987, pp. 9–16.

Hawley, Nell Shapiro and Sohini Sarah Pillai, editors. 'An Introduction to the Literature of the *Mahabharata*.' *Many Mahabharatas*. SUNY Press, 2021, pp. 1–34.

———. 'Manifestations of *Mahabharata*.' Online interview as part of '*Mahabharata*: Conversations' series, Shaw Festival, February 22, 2023.

Knowles, Ric. *Theatre & Interculturalism*. Palgrave Macmillan, 2010.

Lutgendorf, Philip. 'A Long Time Ago in a Galaxy Far, Far Away. *The Mahabharata* as Dystopian Future.' *Many Mahabharatas*, edited by Hawley and Pillai, pp. 361–84.

Pritchett, Frances W. 'The World of Amar Chitra Katha.' *Media and the Transformation of Religion in South Asia*, edited by Lawrence A. Babb and Susan S. Wadley, University of Pennsylvania Press, 1995, pp. 76–106.

Varadpande, M. L. *Mahabharata in Performance*. Clarion Books, 1990.

Williams, David, editor. *Peter Brook and the Mahabharata. Critical Perspectives*. Routledge, 1991.

IN CONVERSATION
WITH THE PLAYWRIGHTS

Karen Fricker and Lawrence Switzky interviewed playwrights and production co-creators Ravi Jain and Miriam Fernandes at the offices of Why Not Theatre in Toronto on April 19, 2023.

Ecology seems very central to the production. It starts and ends with the forest on fire. Is the current climate emergency a framing context for how you're approaching the story?

Miriam Fernandes: Yes. When we did a big rethink in 2021, we came back to three major themes: dharma, storytelling, and ecocide. And ecocide is in the *Mahabharata* already. The reason that Krishna comes to Earth is because the Earth complains to God, saying, 'I'm being destroyed. Humans are killing me. I need your help.' Making ecocide a pillar for us helped us open up the Janamejaya story, which is often used as a framing device for the *Mahabharata*, including ours. The story goes: Janamejaya's father has been killed by a snake, so in order to avenge his father's murder, Janamejaya decides to kill all the snakes in the land. In order to stop this massacre, a storyteller tells him the story of the *Mahabharata*.

Ravi Jain: Lorenzo [Savoini], the set designer, came on the project at the top of 2022, and he connected to Janamejaya's story at the start. He was like, 'That snake story, that's amazing. I'm seeing all these snakes hanging there.'

Over the pandemic, we also met David Suzuki [ed: between 2020 and 2022, Why Not Theatre created the film and theatre production and book *What You Won't Do for Love*, exploring the relationship between love for one's life partner and love for the planet, with Canadian environmental activists David Suzuki and Tara Cullis]. So that stuff is all present in everything we're doing.

How are these environmental questions active in the version of the *Mahabharata* you've arrived at?

MF: In the process of writing the script, we started by trying to bring the story closer to us and our modern world. In the early days, there were contemporary voices and a lot of commentary on the actual stories. In a way, we needed to make the story our own so we could feel that we owned it. In 2018, we wrote what we call the #MeToo script, which was really a contemporary feminist take on the story. It was interesting, but we realized we weren't actually telling the story – we were criticizing it, and we had reduced it. Feminism is in the story, yes, but there was a lot more that the story was trying to speak to. So, after that, our writing process became about removing ourselves from the story. What we do now is tell a distilled version of the *Mahabharata* with the right framing for the audience to make those connections to the modern world themselves.

And the amazing thing is, all these themes are already there. Janamejaya and the snakes are there, the destruction of the Khandava Forest is there, Krishna coming down to Earth because humans are destroying the planet because of greed: it's all there. And it's all 4,000 years old.

What do you think the *Mahabharata* wants us to see about our relationship to the natural, nonhuman world? What is it trying to get us to see about that concern that's pressing right now?

MF: It's what David Suzuki said to us. We need to understand that we're part of a web of relationships, and that's what dharma is. Nothing is fixed. If one thing moves, everything else moves, and we're constantly in relationship to many different things. In every single situation, we need to understand what power and privilege we hold, and accordingly, our responsibility to those beings that have less power and privilege. The Earth is one of those beings.

RJ: *Khana and Kahani* is the place where that gets pulled out the most, because we literally say that. We unpack the story of Yudhishthira by the lake, and Sharada [K Eswar]'s first thing is that the Pandavas have been taking too much from the forest. That's the plight of humans: we take too much, we don't give back. And when you put yourself above others, that's against nature in a way. Animals don't take more than they need; humans take more than they need. Sharada's the one who expands this to nature as part of the web of relationships.

Remember what Devdutt [Pattanaik] said about the story of that young girl who asked, 'Why does Krishna tell Arjuna to burn the trees?' Ultimately, you are in a relationship with nature. In that one instance with the forest, you have to burn it down to achieve a certain thing, but you need to know the cost of that. It's about understanding that you are in relationship to nature. I think *Khana and Kahani* synthesizes that the most.

This understanding that we are in a network of relationships with the land and more-than-human creatures speaks to the current era of decolonization and Indigenous resurgence. Is that part of your conversations?

RJ: It is. Any ancient story, any ancient culture, is going to do that. When the performers go onstage for the first time, they make an offering or a prayer to the stage (see 'Key Terms and Concepts' for a description of *pranam*). It's not about the performer – first, it's the space. And, similarly, with the environment, the relationship to the land is primary. It's about decentring people from the narrative and looking at the whole. Any ancient culture, any first peoples, subscribe to that.

MF: Indigenous people in Canada often talk about making decisions now, with the awareness of how that decision will impact seven generations in the future. And our story starts with Janamejaya, but the Storyteller goes back seven generations. Shantanu is seven generations from Janamejaya. The *Mahabharata* ties in a million different threads of all the choices that not only your parents and your grandparents made, but that seven generations made, that got us to this position. And as we make decisions now, what will be the repercussions of that, and how do we actually think about the impact of that?

We'd like to turn to your approach to casting. Anaka Maharaj-Sandhu, who plays Arjuna, identifies as gender-fluid, which prompts reflection about that character's heroism and the relationship of heroism to gender. How did you arrive at this casting?

RJ: It's practical. When casting, I have a starting place of an idea of who the characters are, and if an individual captures an energy or spirit of the character, then I don't care what gender, ethnicity, or ability they have. I think that they'll unlock something about the character that will be unique to them, interesting, and exciting. I think most actors want to replicate an idea of a character rather than actually doing the hard work of finding themselves in a character. And oftentimes, in an odd way, people find themselves in a character when it's not a character that they would necessarily play because they have no reference point.

Practically, Miriam was playing Arjuna until we rewrote most recently and we thought she should be the Storyteller. Kimberley Rampersad [associate artistic director of the Shaw Festival] said, 'You need to see this person,' who was Anaka. I saw their tape and I thought they were stunning, so I called them and said, 'Hey, do you want to play Arjuna?'

When I started working with Brandy [Leary], the choreographer, she said, 'You know Anaka's six feet tall, right?' I didn't know because we'd met only on Zoom. And who checks just the height on a resumé? Then it became this big boon, because to see Karna played by Navtej [Sandhu], who's also very tall, next to Anaka as Arjuna – it's less about their genders and more about the competition between them, and that said so much more than we could have written.

As with your previous productions, such as *Prince Hamlet*, Ravi, actors are not cast in any uniform or systematic way, so that you seem to be making a comment about the non-essential relationship between a person's race, gender, and ability and the character they might play.

RJ: I'm responding to you using the word *character*. Because the character of a person is not solely their identity. Identity informs my character, but my character is something deeper. If we think about character in this way, we go deeper than what are, in a lot of ways, superficial identities, that have nothing and everything to do with my character.

When you work with actors, it's not about erasing. It's not about neutral – that anybody can play anything. It's actually the opposite. It has to do with the specificity of the collision of, for example, Navtej and Karna. And it has more to do with revealing Navtej's Navtej-ness and Karna's Karna-ness, finding the meeting point of that. That's what reveals a different kind of Karna than we're used to seeing, than the idea of Karna that many people have. He's a made-up character. What makes those characters so human is that we actually see the actors behind them.

You mentioned what you're calling the #MeToo version of the script. How did conversations evolve about how to handle the things that happen in *Mahabharata* that are bad for women?

MF: In that #MeToo version, the characters of 'Ravi' and 'Miriam' were the framing device: Ravi was telling the story and Miriam was listening to it and challenging the story. The conversation between the two storytellers came to a head around the disrobing of Draupadi story. Miriam's text was something like, 'I don't want to hear this story again, why are we telling these stories if nothing changes?' The challenge with that was, by doing that, we discredited everything else in the story. We were being really clever and really contemporary and saying we're really smart and woke. But actually, the story is way more complicated, and the world is way more complicated than that. The conversations about what happens to women and what happens to people of a lower class – all of that is there already. What we try to find in this version is how we create the space to be in that problem together. In the #MeToo version, the Ravi and Miriam characters solved the problem for us. We said, 'That's bad.' We all can agree that it's bad and leave the theatre and feel good about ourselves, as opposed to really being in the problem.

In the text, in Draupadi's monologue, she puts us all in a problem we've all been in, when we are in rooms with people in power who do problematic things. We are complicit.

RJ: We all do that. We're in rooms and later we go, 'Why the f— didn't I say anything?' You think about it after and you don't know why. You just are silent. So, it's about getting people to really sit in the reality and not justify, not solve, not make their character a good person or have a reason for doing or not doing something.

MF: And not force a clear trajectory. In linear storytelling, my character goes from here to there. In real life, we don't do that. Ravi, you said this to me a long time ago, when actors say, 'My character wouldn't say that.' Ravi said, 'I say and do things that I would never do all the time. I don't want to, but I do it.' And I think that's the amazing thing that I discovered when we finally surrendered to the complexity of the stories: it is life. Life is that complicated and that messy, and we're not used to seeing that in theatre.

How does the current staging of the disrobing of Draupadi hold that complexity?

MF: Goldy [Notay], the actor playing Draupadi, started using the whole audience. She's speaking to this hall of men and she's asking, 'Where's dharma in this hall? Where is justice? How can we allow this to happen?' Now she's not just talking to the twelve actors on stage, she's speaking to the whole space. Being onstage, I get emotional in that scene. When else in our world does someone get to stand onstage in front of 800 people and get to speak that truth?

In our conversation with Jay Emmanuel [who plays Shiva, Amba, Drupada, and Pandu], he said that he finds the production very queer, because there's no attempt to define what a man or a woman is, what the characters' sexuality or gender are (see page 172). As he sees it, you can't do *Mahabharata* if you're stuck to binary ways of thinking. We're wondering how this sits with you.

RJ: I like that description, but the approach wasn't necessarily to define it as queer. For me, it's part of how I like to tell classical stories, in that they are contemporary and ancient at once. Design-wise, we talked a lot about that, particularly with the costumes. They don't really evolve as the set evolves and becomes more contemporary. The idea was to make sure that we weren't ever placing it in a 'now.' That was the one major hurdle for some of the actors – what time are we in? Where are we? I really resisted them defining that. Just be in the story, whatever that is. You are a contemporary body and a contemporary person, so it's contemporary. It's an ancient story, so it's ancient. It's both.

In the second half of the show, technology enters the staging: you bring in cameras and feeds and projections. We recall that there was always a technological component – at one point, you were going to have an audio tour of a forest in between the two halves, or a VR element, or something that people could play in their cars on their way down to the Shaw Festival. We're curious how that evolved into the second half of the show.

RJ: Those ideas were born out of fear and out of a desire to cover up because I didn't have a handle on the story. They were cool ideas to try to make up for a lack.

What's unique for me about the way the technology works now – and all the storytelling, in fact – is that it was born out of the workshop process. We found the use of video by fluke because in the July 2019 workshop, [video designer] Hana Kim was in the room for the first time. She had all this gear and she said, 'Why don't we try this?' And I loved it. It matched the text that we had, it drew me into it, it created an energy that helped me hear and feel the scene. So it became this touchpoint, but we had to figure out why it was there.

Then COVID happened, and we also changed design teams, and we would battle a little bit because I was holding on to formal approaches to how we needed to tell the story. Lorenzo and Gillian [Gallow], two amazing designers, just started asking great questions. Lorenzo was the one to help clarify and articulate what the evolution of media in the show was going to be and why.

Hana had a source image that was like a war room because I had told her, 'Let's look at images of war over time.' Lorenzo ran with that: 'What if it's this makeshift war room that they set up in the palace?'

We're wondering where you place yourself in a tradition of directing, Ravi, that includes Peter Brook and Robert Wilson and Robert Lepage. We see you fitting into a tradition of staging spectacle.

RJ: I think those three are my teachers … and [Simon] McBurney, all those guys. I will also throw this idea of spectacle back to Lorenzo. He's the one who was like, 'And these chandeliers come in.' I had never done that before. I had never had the resources for that or the verticality to play with. Ultimately, I had never had a stage this big, so you've got to hit it out of the park. With Lorenzo, I talked a lot about the design having to be epic. I knew we were starting with fire, so we needed the opposite. We have to go to the contrast, so that the fire will mean something.

MF: It's a lot of Hana Kim's work, too, in that spectacle, and [lighting designer] Kevin Lamotte.

RJ: And Crystal [Lee], our production manager. Shaw had never had such complex video design in its sixty-year history.

This feels like a typical deflection: you're saying it's about others when we're saying it's about you, Ravi.

RJ: I'm the filter because I'm filtering all the conversations. You know how when you run, you'll run at the pace the other person's running at. If you're faster than me, I'll have to catch up. And there was an element of that on this team. Everyone was just pushing.

You've spoken about how formative seeing Peter Brook's *Mahabharata* was for you twenty years ago. What specifically do you remember that shaped you as a director?

RJ: I had been a big fan for a long time; I saw his *Hamlet*, and I saw *The Suit*, a number of shows in New York and Toronto. And when I saw the film of *Mahabharata*, I just thought the actors were so interesting. He took the unfamiliar and made it very familiar for me, because I kind of knew it. I was blown away and amazed at how simple it all seemed. And I've always been a fan of his essentialization, and that's something I steal from a lot in his work.

What do you mean by essentialization?

RJ: *(Mimes holding a stem.)* This is a flower. I love you, and it smells as beautiful as you. *(Mimes again.)* I can give you the flower. Without having the flower there, those gestures essentialize the interaction, the relationship, and the exchange more than the object. But in a weird way, in doing that, it reveals the object even more. In so much of Brook's work, there is the space that is empty, but also filled. I love that. Then I read Rustom [Bharucha]'s article [critiquing Brook's *Mahabharata*] and I started learning and thinking differently about race and appropriation.

What was it about Brook's company in Paris that interested you?

RJ: A centre for international theatre research and creation: having the resource and the space to bring people together from different backgrounds and experiences to explore what a universal story is or what storytelling is. This is controversial, but I don't think we could have done this production with a Canadian cast only, because the breadth of stage experience elevated the room – the difference in understanding what theatre can be that came from geographical experiences, life experiences.

Miriam, seeing you as the Storyteller is new to this version. What's your relationship to the action in *Karma*?

MF: I feel that I'm conducting. The story is happening, but I'm the conduit for everything happening. So most cues are taken from me. The band and I are working together, so that it should feel that the whole story comes from me. That was part of the original vision: all of this story, all of this spectacularity, comes from one person speaking to an audience, and the imagination that they plant in that audience.

Does the Storyteller have a relationship or a reaction to the story? It strikes us that you're not a neutral participant.

MF: I felt that throughout the whole process. Every day I felt I was listening to the story and being affected by it.

RJ: We couldn't figure out what it was. And then there was one day where we did a run. And you were like, 'I got it. I just figured it out. I'm Vyasa, and these are my ancestors. This is the story I'm telling you, to warn you to not do this, because it happened to me.'

MF: It started becoming really clear to me in the Amba backstory with Bhishma: at the end of Jay's dance as Amba, he throws ash up into the air, symbolizing Amba jumping into the fire. I watch it, saying to myself, 'I'm going to let her hang in the air right now. I'll come back to her in Part Two, in five hours.' That's what's going on in my head. I opened up that thread for you, and I'm going to come back to it. I have to craft that for the audience so that they can follow.

To me, the greatest success as the Storyteller is at the end of the play after Yudhishthira says, 'What's the point? There's no future. All our kids are dead.' Krishna says, 'I spared one child. He lives in the belly of Uttara.' And I say, 'The widow of Abhimanyu, that child, he'll grow to rule for future generations until he's killed by a snake named Takshaka.' And the whole audience reacts. If you've seen the whole show in one day, you haven't heard that name for five or seven hours. If you saw the show over two days, you haven't heard it for at least twenty-four or forty-eight hours. But the fact that people remember who that snake is, that's amazing.

A CONVERSATION ON MYTHS
AND STORYTELLING

Devdutt Pattanaik is a mythologist based in Mumbai, India. His book, Jaya, *was a source for this production of* Mahabharata. *Karen Fricker and Lawrence Switzky spoke with Pattanaik, Miriam Fernandes, and Ravi Jain.*

The concept of a clash of cultures is central to how you explain the relationship between East and West, Devdutt. Ravi and Miriam, how did this concept shape your vision for your *Mahabharata*?

Ravi Jain: Around 2010, I saw Devdutt's TED Talk 'East vs. West – the myths that mystify,' and it blew me away. It spoke to me so deeply because I grew up in Canada in a culturally Indian home. Many of the confusing interactions that Devdutt describes in his talk are things I lived and experienced. With *Mahabharata* specifically, the approach I took from the start was, well, of course I'm Indian, but I don't feel Indian. I'm Canadian, but I also don't feel Canadian. I'm this hybrid strange thing, and there are many of me out there. So how do I approach and tell this story that is so Indian, so important to Hindu culture?

The first choice we made immediately was to make this production with a diaspora cast. All of these people have a connection to India, but maybe they grew up in Australia or Malaysia or in the north of England or in Winnipeg. All the collisions of who we are would be infused in how we approach the storytelling and how we bring ourselves to it.

Devdutt, how do you respond to what you're hearing about how these ideas about the clash of cultures are being staged in this production?

Devdutt Pattanaik: I love the way it's presented. Visually, the show is very stark. Many Indians have seen this story on television with lots of costumes, and the costumes can be very distracting. I love the simplicity of it here. When you have a very simple set and very few people onstage using minimal props, it helps you focus on what is trying to be told.

Ravi and Miriam, could you talk more about how you're approaching the show from a storytelling and staging perspective?

Miriam Fernandes: The show is meant to take you on a journey. It's like you take a taxi to the airport, then you take a plane, then you take a boat, then you go on an underwater submarine – all these different forms of transportation are like the different forms of storytelling that we use. We searched hard to find the right vehicle for each part of the story. We start in a really ancient way with a storyteller and audience around a fire. That evolves into simple storytelling in the world of street theatre, where I put down a stool and somebody stands on that stool, and that makes them the king. From there, we grow into scenes, technology emerges, and huge videos and projections take over, until eventually all the technology fails, and we come back to a fire.

Eastern and Western storytelling traditions are always both present as well. It doesn't feel like we're ever just in one or the other. There are Eastern forms like Odissi and Kathakali which the performers brought into the room. But even when you see that Kathakali, it's a clash of traditional Kathakali storytelling, and Kathak and contemporary dance … it's a collision of forms.

RJ: What's important for me as a storyteller is to find a way to unlock the meaning of it. Miriam and I, we kept saying, *how* we tell the story is the key to unlocking its meaning. That's why the middle portion of our telling is a meal. It's sitting with an auntie or a didi, a sister, who tells you a story over food, and she not only tells the story, but tries to unpack its meaning.

DP: The storytelling doesn't exist for the story. It exists for the people listening to the story. It's the audience that is most important. The storyteller exists for the audience. In India, all wisdom is considered to be contained in this body of work called the Vedas, which means knowledge. Every human being is confused about life, and all answers are in the Vedas. But the Vedas are too complicated. And so they say, let's turn it into a story. That story is called the *Mahabharata*.

The theatre is a communication tool, and in India, the stage is a sacred space. Many Indian artists, when they climb on the stage, they will pray to the stage. You're entering a sacred space and you become what is called a patra – that is the word for actor. *Patra* means a vessel. You are the vessel through which the idea is going to reach the audience.

You have to do whatever it takes so that the audience gets the idea. It's like serving food. If your audience cannot digest a particular kind of food, you will change it, change the spices so that you match the digestive capacity of your audience. So if it's an English audience, you will do it in English. A Chinese audience, you will do it in Chinese. You are serving food that will give nourishment to your audience so that when they leave, they burp in satisfaction. In the very best circumstance they go back nourished, healed.

MF: Your voice has flowed through us, Devdutt, and your passion for the accessibility of the story. We use a piece of your book *Jaya* at the beginning of the play. We say, 'Do not be confused by the plots: within this forest of stories flows a river of wisdom.' You can feel that everybody comes in with this tension of having to figure out this whole story. So many people have said that line sticks with them, and it lets them just keep experiencing it because it's not something to be understood in a day.

Devdutt, can you talk about your understanding of karma and dharma, which are so central to *Mahabharata*?

DP: In South Asian ideas, rebirth plays a very important role. Rebirth can be seen as real – like, I'm born again and again and again. It can be also seen as an abstraction, that every event is caused by something and leads to something else. So every event is the fruit of the seed of the past, and every event is the seed of the future.

Karma basically means that. Whether you like it or not, there are seeds and fruit, seeds and fruit. If humans didn't exist, karma would still exist because animals and birds and the cycle of life are going on. In the forest, there is an animal that is hungry, and it eats. A tiger will eat a deer. Does that make the tiger a villain? Disney will make it into a villain. But the predator is hungry, it wants to eat, it'll eat the deer, and that's karma. The hungry will eat. There is the eater and the eaten. There are no heroes, there are no villains. There are no victims in nature.

Humans come into the picture, and humans are different because we are not just looking for food. We are looking for respect, we're looking for attention, we are looking for power. Our hunger never ends. We can keep on eating. We want more and more. That's something peculiar to humans. The question comes: how should humans behave? From that comes dharma. Humans don't just eat and be eaten like animals. I can feed you, and you can be fed. You can expect someone to take care of you, and people will expect you to take care of them.

That's empathy, and that's what makes us human. We can't expect that of animals or plants. We expect of humans that you have to be helpful to people: I have to help you, and I hope you will help me. That's all dharma is. That's what makes you human.

People in the West use the word *karma* as a synonym for *justice*: 'Oh, karma will get to you.' People use this biblical line: 'As you sow, so you reap.' That's not a line from the *Gita*. The *Gita* says you have control over only your actions, not the results. You can sow anything, but we don't know what you will reap. Krishna is saying your power is in the sowing, not the reaping.

Can you be empathetic when shit is happening to you? Can you be kind on a battlefield? That's what Krishna is trying to say. If you don't fight your cousins, they will keep oppressing and they will keep being corrupt. You can't allow that to happen because then society will collapse. But in the process of hurting them, in the process of killing them, you are being cursed too. You are going to hurt a lot of people, there's going to be a lot of collateral damage. But you have to accept it because you have to understand how society works. It requires a lot of stoic energy to walk onto the battlefield knowing that nobody's a bad guy.

How do you explain all this in a simple story to a child? If I'm going to explain to a child, I create this story of rich cousins, poor cousins, the burning of the forests, resource management. Today we're talking about climate change, social inequality, toxic nationalism. Same things, the same questions.

RJ: We met Devdutt in the pandemic over Zoom, and he talked about hoarding toilet paper and what a fiasco that was. The clarity of his presentation of the ideas really simplified this complex story for us. A lot of people who've seen our *Mahabharata* will be like, 'Oh wow, Ukraine.' And I go, 'Yes, and also, when you were driving and you got cut off and you wanted to cut them off even more.' The battle is inside us, it's challenging ourselves to really reflect on our attachment to revenge and anger.

MF: Yesterday there was an eight-year-old girl who waited for me in the lobby to ask me a question. She said, 'I thought Krishna was a good guy, but then why did he tell Arjuna to burn down the forest? That's not good.' And I said, 'Yes, that's the right question.' Why does Krishna do all these things in the war, and Arjuna, and Bhima? From a western storytelling perspective, we're not used to the contradictions of characters and the very complex morality in this story.

DP: Through westernization, people are using words like *good, bad, right, wrong*, without understanding context. What is good for you could be terrible for someone else. Good for whom? Nobody's asked that. They make it objective. Clash of cultures is that. It's moving out of the assumption of objectivity.

This child has been told cutting forests is bad. And the child doesn't realize that the lifestyle that the child is living is the outcome of many forests being burned. The children don't realize that milk comes by milking a cow; milk doesn't magically appear. You have to take away the cow's freedom, and all your privileges are the outcome. All privileges, not just white privilege, are the outcome of taking something from someone else – that is something that humans can't handle. Even Krishna could not stop the war. Even Krishna is helpless in front of egomaniacs.

The irony of it is something that we all forget. When I was being attacked by [online] trolls at one time, I was getting very mad. But then I read in my own writings: you can control what you sow, but you can't control what you reap. Even Krishna cannot control what he reaps: it applies to him and it applies to all of us. You and I don't know what this conversation will lead to, or what your production will lead to. We can only focus on doing a good job and hopefully with empathy.

IN CONVERSATION
WITH THE PERFORMERS

Jay Emmanuel is an actor, director, and Kathakali dancer based in Perth, Australia. He plays Shiva, Amba, Drupada, and Pandu in the production.

What was your relationship to *Mahabharata* before this production?

Jay Emmanuel: I grew up with it because of my training in Kathakali and because I was brought up in India. *Mahabharata* was on television, grandmas tell the stories, it's in the festivals. All of life is built around the *Mahabharata*.

Kathakali was basically built for the *Mahabharata*. Because we had this massive story, which is 4,000 years old. And Kathakali is about 400, 500 years old. And the thing is, in India, we were going, 'How do we tell these epic stories?' And from that came a form. It's intertwined.

How did Ravi and Miriam find out about your training in Kathakali?

JE: It happened in an early workshop. Miriam and I were asked to devise a scene of the war. Literal representation did not interest me, and it didn't interest Ravi and Miriam either. We wanted to investigate abstraction. What does war move like? How do we create that? How do we cut through to the essence of war? Even with 14, or 100, or 200 bodies, it's impossible to put war onstage. And then I remember there was an improvisation where I was like, 'Okay, I'm not going to use any words. I'm just going to move.' And Meher [Pavri, opera singer] was singing on top of it, and it was one of the most magical moments.

How close to what you originally devised is the movement in this production?

JE: It's much more detailed. Back then, there were influences coming from contemporary dance. But by the time we reached the production, we had to settle on a form. What you see onstage is almost word for word storytelling in Kathakali, including some things that are not in the script. Kathakali is like a language: people who know Indian classical dance are able to read what's happening.

For example, we don't have a mudra (see 'Key Terms and Concepts') for the character of Shikhandi in *Dharma*, the reincarnation of princess Amba from *Karma*. Shikhandi is a man and a woman, and they are a big question even in the history of our performance forms. We haven't given them a name in Kathakali. We don't even have a gesture for them. So in this show, we had to create gestures and language for things that had never existed. I had to go back to the big school of Kathakali in Kerala and I had to ask a few different people, how do you create some of the stories that we are telling in this *Mahabharata*?

What advice did you get?

JE: In the context of where Kathakali is, of where classical performance is now, there was a sense of flexibility. In Kathakali, there are about 400 stories out of which are twenty we tell regularly. It's a repertoire – you repeat them. In this *Mahabharata*, there are new parts of *Mahabharata* that we are creating completely new Kathakali choreography for. And there was a lot of generosity, from the school, from my gurus: 'Hey, go ahead. We need this, because otherwise the form will die.' Perhaps it's the start of a new repertoire in a form that's so old.

What other contributions have you made to this *Mahabharata*?

JE: Early in the creation process, I was the only person who had lived in India. I knew what relationship people had to *Mahabharata*. At the very beginning, we were still trying to find out what a modern retelling of *Mahabharata* means. What issues are we going to deal with? Do we need to bring in references from today? Do we need to make them explicit?

It was a journey of finding the trust to let *Mahabharata* say what you need to say, because it's timeless. So I think to find that faith in it – I feel very deeply about that. That it's better to leave it as is, to keep it neutral. And I think that led to us finding the tone, which still reverberates with our modern sensibilities.

I'm also a deviser, and I love physical devising. I went to the École internationale de théâtre Jacques Lecoq in Paris. That was another attempt to find a way of bridging two different worlds, theatre and dance. In India, you bring everything together to tell the story: the acting, the dance, the singing, the mudras, all of it. In this production, there was a huge conversation around that. We need to bring everything together rather than keeping things separate. In the Lecoq way, which is also Ravi and Miriam's training, we could devise, we could play.

I also really pushed to highlight the queerness in the work. That was really important for me, because in India it's so rare that you see it. I felt a responsibility to my queer brothers and my dance community.

The whole production is actually incredibly queer. There are no boundaries. There's no trying to define what a man or a woman is – or their sexuality, even. When you look really closely into the production, inside each character, you'll find queerness. You can't do *Mahabharata* if you're stuck in binary ways of thinking. It goes, 'No, there's not just this and that, there is all of it.' And that's queerness, because it can't be defined.

Many of the characters that you're playing in *Mahabharata* give themselves over to anger and destruction. Do you see your roles as related?

JE: There's a bloodline of revenge. It passes through all the characters I play except Pandu. And it's actually very satisfying to be part of that bloodline and to carry it across the production. Amba reaches out to Shiva. Shikhandi is a child of Shiva. Drupada prays to Shiva. We realized during the development that I gravitated toward these characters. Revenge keeps the stories going forward. How do I deal with it? It's been very challenging because they come onstage, you see a flash of it, and then they disappear.

An audience member said to me, 'The dance of Drupada in *Karma* sets the tone for the next half.' That character is there for about two minutes and then dances for three minutes. But it sets the tone of revenge, the weight, the density that only something made of that dance and that theatricality can bring to the table.

Speaking of dancing, the dance you perform as Shiva in *Dharma* is extraordinary in terms of its velocity and stamina. How do you prepare for that?

JE: Before I started my run in this production, my instinct was, 'Jay, you need to go to India and nourish yourself there.' And I went to Kerala, where Kathakali was born. It's the one place you'll see *Mahabharata* every week if you want to. Almost every day at certain points. I just went deep for two months in this. I was living in *Mahabharata*. I was training. It inspired me to see different versions of Shiva, to see different versions of Krishna, to see different versions of each character.

And it wasn't just about doing this production; it's something bigger than this production. I certainly thought about the monumental task of playing a god in *Mahabharata* – what does it mean for a human being to do that in their lifetime? How many people in this world ever get a chance to do this?

Is the makeup and hair in your presentation of Shiva traditional?

JE: Some elements of it are, but the costume is not. For this production, we knew that Shiva needed to move a lot. Kathakali is performed on a rectangular stage and it's very small. Because the space has changed in this production, we also needed to change the form. The image of the circle played a big part from the beginning. In developing the war in *Dharma* through improvisation, we found the circle. And then Ravi carried it back into *Karma*. In our conversations and discussions of *Mahabharata*, we said, 'Life is very circular, it just moves around. What goes around comes back around.' And that's karma.

The costume needed to change because the movement had changed. In Kathakali, because you don't spin, you can have this big costume. But now that we wanted spinning to be a part of it, we needed to keep only the parts that helped this movement.

And there was a requirement, dramaturgically, that Shiva move between different characters. I appear as Shiva, but then I become Shik-handi, and I become Abhimanyu, the son of Arjuna. Even inside of Shiva, you're playing three or four character shifts, and you're even playing the elephant Ashwatthama. It meant that the costume needed to be neutral enough for me to move into different characters.

᳚

Anaka Maharaj-Sandu is an actor based in Winnipeg, Canada, who plays Arjuna. Goldy Notay is an actor based in London, England, who plays Gandhari and Draupadi. Ellora Patnaik is an actor and Odissi dancer based in Toronto, Canada, who plays Kunti and Drona.

Could each of you talk about your relationship to *Mahabharata* before this production? Has it always been part of your life?

Goldy Notay: I was once cast as Draupadi in a play called *Panchali*, which was based on her relationship with her five husbands. So that was my first introduction to Draupadi, but I didn't really know anything about the *Mahabharata*. Years later, I was doing my yoga teacher training and that's when I was illuminated by the *Bhagavad Gita*. And so I just had little snapshots of the *Mahabharata*. I didn't grow up in a family where everyone told me a story. I mentioned my lack of expertise to Ravi when I first met him, but thankfully that didn't faze him from having me step into the fold.

Anaka Maharaj-Sandu: I am also by no means an expert, but my maternal grandparents are quite religious and passed on their knowledge to me at a young age. I was also introduced to the *Mahabharata* as a kid through the children's *Mahabharata* books and the very dramatic soap operas on Indian TV, and the *Gita* and things like that were always kicking around. The soap operas were always on at a grandma's house.

Ellora Patnaik: I was born and raised with the *Mahabharata*. One of the first images I remember was Krishna's statue in my mother's altar at home. We're not a particularly religious family, but all art from India is based in the religion and the spirituality of the country.

Ellora, can you tell us about your background in dance and how that came to feature so prominently in this production through the character of Kunti?

EP: My mother is an Indian classical dancer, now retired, an Odissi dancer. It's one of the main classical dances of India – the same style of dancing that I do – originally from the state my parents were from, Odisha.

The storytelling – *abhinaya* – in classical dance is communicated through facial expression and hand gestures. Content from *Mahabharata* is present throughout all forms of Indian classical dance, and is very common in all the traditional repertoire.

I actually didn't expect it to have so much time onstage. When Ravi came to me with the offer, I thought we were just doing Kalaripayattu, the

Indian martial art that our choreographer, Brandy Leary, brought to the show. Especially playing Drona, I thought I was going to be doing Kalari.

And the day before I moved to Niagara for the workshops and premiere of *Mahabharata*, Ravi and I had a Zoom call and said, 'Hey, buddy, what do you think about dancing?' And I said, 'Yeah, you mean the Kalari, right?' He said, 'No, I was thinking about Odissi.' I'd been teaching all through the pandemic on Zoom, but I haven't danced onstage for some time. I didn't feel I was up for it. But for Kunti we took the softer style of dance, what we call the Lasya. I saw Jay's take on Shiva, and I thought this would be a nice counterpoint. He's doing a lot of the Tandava, which stands for Shiva and the stronger, more rigorous style of dance, whereas Lasya is supple and fluid. It was fitting for the birth of the Pandavas.

I was happy about the classical elements – particularly Odissi – in this production because it's a dying form. It's dying even in India. There's a very select audience that wants to hear classical anything, whether it's classical music or ballet in this country. But there are people who, if it's presented in the right way, with Western theatrics the way we do it here – they might not get it completely but they can appreciate the aesthetics of it and the visuals and how it caters to the story.

Goldy, Draupadi's stories in *Mahabharata* are well known and pivotal, but some of that material is challenging for contemporary audiences. Draupadi is married to all five Pandavas, and she is disrobed. How did you begin to think about playing her?

GN: I was petrified about having to play Draupadi, which I mentioned to Ravi. But then I just received it as one of those great life challenges. I didn't want to victimize her in any way, and tried to imbue her with a modern-day sensibility about one's body and their ownership of it in a world that is fundamentally run by men. I thought, how can we find a way of showing believable defiance toward the disrobing, while allowing the authenticity of the story to unfold? Ravi always reminded me that Draupadi was other-worldly (she was birthed out of fire), so that helped to give her a distinctive voice. I think everything – the #MeToo movement, everything that I've ever felt as a woman – has enabled me to craft her. Ravi and I also made a decision to give her some agency in her swayamvara (see 'Key Terms and Concepts'), where she selects her husband. But because she's so iconic, one is given an impossible task. You can never appeal to everyone. I just had to make some bold decisions, and reciprocally, Draupadi enabled me to find bravery in telling her tale.

Anaka, what do you want audiences to see in your Arjuna, another well-known character, that maybe they haven't encountered before?

AMS: Well, Arjuna is a very dignified character, and he's a demigod. He's the greatest archer in the world. And so I think it's easy to lose the human aspect of him and the fact that he is flawed and the fact that he has a massive ego. The important thing for me is to think, how do I meet that? And at the same time, I'm none of those things and none of us are any of those things.

I had to let go of trying to make him this incredibly otherworldly being, because we're putting this on in a theatre for people, and what people want to see is characters that they can relate to and characters that they identify with. Grounding him in the human world was very important to me because even in the soaps that I know, the way that these characters are represented is very godly and usually shirtless. I wanted to bring it back to the human and to think about how I can identify with him and how everyone else can identify with him.

Are there specific moments in your performance that accentuate Arjuna's humanness?

AMS: The story of Ekalavya in *Karma* is a big one. Arjuna is complicit in elitism and privilege and he doesn't say anything. Arjuna lets Drona cut off this boy's finger because he wants to be the greatest archer in the world. Also the disrobing of Draupadi: he sits there and he does not do anything. That's a moment that was also hard for me. I asked myself, 'Okay, why did he not say anything?' And you can try to excuse him with, 'Well, it's his older brother doing it and he's the king and you can't really challenge that.' But that was a hard thing to grapple with.

I sometimes found it a lot easier to say, 'He's just a man.' And there is, in our society, a lack of respect in the way that men view women. Historically that's also been the case. And so Arjuna asks us to acknowledge that and ask, is it true that he couldn't have done anything? I think he could have done more. I looked for moments like that. There are a lot of moments where he makes choices that are flawed. But a lot of other people would've done the same things because of ego or because of pride or not wanting to embarrass himself in front of a hall full of men.

One of the joys of this production is seeing you all play so many different roles. What are the challenges and the pleasures of moving between characters?

EP: It's a delight for somebody who wants to be fast on their feet as an actor. It's a marathon for me backstage because we're like Superman: we're tearing off our shirts as we run offstage and the wigs are flying and the beads are flying and I'm putting on earrings. I love the contrasts. It's also choices of where I let my voice sit and how I distinguish between them through looks and glances. Even just relaxing my brow: I make Drona quite the grump with my frown. I'm going to have added wrinkles after this.

There's also a strong gender distinction between my characters. Drona is born a man. He's Brahmin, he's very straight and composed. Kunti is like – words fly out of her mouth and she's distressed. And she's got this curse that she's living with. And so there are different head spaces for the two. I always believe in working from the outside in and on how they ground themselves. I play Drona very, very still.

GN: The challenges were also the pleasures. I wanted to find contrasts between them. I worked with the ground a lot as Gandhari. Her fertility (she has 100 sons) ends with losing her children in the earth of a battlefield. And when her son, Duryodhana, died, I said to Ravi, 'I want her to relinquish her wealth, her gold, her crown and be on the ground, in the dirt with him.' You don't ever see royals on their knees, so we had Gandhari mourning in the soil. And with Draupadi, because she's born from fire, I wanted to keep her very upright, so she's always sort of rising. The flame is flickering, the embers alight. Gandhari is a seeker of peace, albeit a questionable one. And Draupadi is a fighter for peace, a warrior, despite the consequences. So one was seated, more servile, while the other was like a women's rights protester. The costume changes were a challenge and initially terrifying, but over time, the terror turned into rhythmic glee! And I could move in and out of the two characters with ease.

This production of *Mahabharata* is notable for the way actors aren't necessarily cast in roles that match their gender. Anaka, can you

talk about how you're experiencing this as a gender-fluid person playing Arjuna?

AMS: I was surprised when Ravi called me to play Arjuna. I think that even for someone who's as distant from gender as possible, you still have conceptions of what people are supposed to look like or what people look like in your head. All of these are strong men with their long hair and their moustaches.

Even just from talking to a lot of audience members, they don't care. We're playing demigods. If they weren't going to buy into this, they would not be buying into it from the first five minutes. It's not going to be me playing Arjuna that takes them out of the story, or Ellora playing Drona that's going to take them out of the story. They buy it regardless of who's in the role.

My girlfriend actually told me yesterday that someone in the audience said, 'I think Arjuna is a nonbinary actor and that's so cool.' Clearly someone else was touched by that and has a similar life experience. So it's really nice to hear that and the other audience members being like, 'Wow, at first I thought you were a guy and then I thought you were a girl and then I didn't really care.' Having those conversations has been great because I think we need to give the audience more credit – that they are with us and that they want to support us. And that as long as you're being honest and genuine and who you are, then they'll buy into it.

IN CONVERSATION
WITH THE MUSICIANS

Suba Sankaran is the co-creator of the original music and sound design for Maha-bharata *along with John Gzowski. Suba is the Band Leader and a performer in the live band of* Part 1: Karma. *She is a composer and musician based in Toronto, Canada.*

How did you get involved with this production?

Suba Sankaran: It was 2017 or '18 when John Gzowski approached me. He was already on board as sound designer and composer. He knew that he wanted to find a co–sound designer and co-composer who had a foot in the West and a foot in the East, to be true to where the *Mahabharata* comes from in terms of the traditional music, be it South Indian Carnatic music or North Indian Hindustani music. It was only later that we figured out that we were going to have a live band in the first half, and in the second half do it all as pre-recorded sound design.

Can you talk about how *Mahabharata* has figured in your life?

SS: I was born and raised in Toronto. My father is a famous master drummer named Trichy Sankaran, the founder of South Indian Music Studies at York University in Toronto. I started doing South Indian singing, drumming, and vocal percussion from about the age of two onwards. I started singing in choirs at four or five, started piano at six, and it went on from there.

On sabbatical, my father would take our family to South India where he and my mom were born. I remember when I was eight years old, you'd hear singing and these really big, regal, superhero kind of sounds blaring from whoever had a television. The *Mahabharata* TV series was the call for people to gather in those homes around dinnertime.

I followed the series when I was there. I can understand both Tamil and Telugu, my mother tongue, so I knew what was happening. On top of that, one of my uncles used to write for and illustrate the *Mahabharata* comic books. So I did grow up with those stories, and because I was study-ing South Indian classical singing, which is all devotional music, I would also get some of the stories through those songs.

Could you talk about the relationship of composed music to improvisation in *Karma*?

ss: John and I came into the rehearsal process in January [2023] with some musical cues and songs. Once we got there, there was a healthy debate, because you already have actors who are telling the story. You don't really need the musicians to add more text to further the story. So nearly all the songs we wrote were abbreviated. What was an actual song with verses and a chorus became one line. It's such a humbling experience as a composer. You don't want to be too precious.

For all the musicians, but specifically me and Hasheel [Lodhia] because we have a lot of experience in both Hindustani and classical Carnatic music, there were certain ragas [ed: ragas or raags are melodic frameworks for improvisation] that each of us has chosen throughout *Karma*. One of the ragas that I use at the very end of *Karma* is one that's meant for the early morning, because the dawn of battle is happening – or exile, whatever you want to call it, but it feels like something is starting fresh.

Every raga has what they call a rasa, which is a mood. The music we use for the wedding and other celebratory scenes, it's a specific kind of raga that's said to induce joy and laughter. It's auspicious as well, so it's meant to be celebratory and also sacred.

We ended up choosing a lot of these ragas, finding melodic motifs that became their own mini-songs. But beyond that, it's all improvised, and because all the musicians are consummate improvisers, it's amazing. No day will be the same. Everybody's getting a brand-new experience, including us.

What kinds of conversations have you been having with audiences in the lobby after performances?

ss: I'm always a bit surprised how much they appreciate the music. And a lot of them don't know that the musicians aren't in the second half, so that comes as a huge shock.

Many people have said that the music is well-balanced, that it fits in with all the right subtle nuances to further the action onstage. For me, that's a compliment of the highest sort. Many people have said that they love how Ravi and Miriam have distilled all the stories and picked the ones that they want to represent, because there are a million of them. It's just good storytelling in the end – that's what people have said. They say it's sort of epic on epic on epic.

ﻪﻠﻋ

Hasheel Lodhia is the traditional music consultant for Mahabharata. *He performs in the live band of Part 1:* Karma, *playing the bansuri, among many other instruments. Hasheel is a musician based in Toronto, Canada.*

At what stage of the process did you join this production?

Hasheel Lodhia: I joined in 2018, with another musician – we were the only musicians in the room at that point. There was no real process; we were just asked to bring our instruments and bring ourselves. It was a lot of storytelling, and we were jamming along.

Apart from my voice and my flutes, I brought a variety of percussion instruments. This is my first theatre production, so I was like, 'Okay, let's just see. I'm sure there are going to be lots of sound effects.' So we had little finger cymbals, tambourines, a kalimba, conch, and other instruments.

Is your training and background in classical Indian music?

HL: It is in North Indian music – Hindustani classical music. I've been training since I was three years old, so thirty years of training almost full-time.

I was born in Canada and my dad was my first teacher. I did most of my lessons in Canada, but after high school I went to India for a year and studied a bit more professionally. I learned with some of the great masters, and now my teachers are in India. There are a handful of bansuri players in North America.

On average I do forty-five shows a year, and they are one-offs; I'm not used to playing the same thing more than once. So to do a show night after night at the Shaw Festival was something very different for me.

What is the texture of the music in *Karma*? What do you hope audiences listen for?

HL: We've designed the music with the idea that it's great if you pick up on things, but it's also okay if you don't. We've dedicated certain raags and certain compositions to different characters, and there are instruments that are related to certain characters. We really think the music helps make this story less confusing because we're always referencing things that happened. There's this sense of 'Okay, there's an emotional memory from the past scene,' even if they can't exactly remember what happened earlier.

Is there anything about the music in *Karma* that you particularly love? Are there moments you really look forward to?

HL: I definitely look forward to the birth of the Pandavas because that scene is one of the fuller classical pieces that I get to play. It's the longest time we're playing one raag. It's a big challenge for me overall in the show to be switching raags every minute because it can ordinarily take thirty minutes to develop the note structure and the mood of a certain raag. In the birth of the Pandavas, because we've stuck to one simple scale and we do it throughout the whole dance, I get to dig deeper into that raag. We do a lot of raag Todi as well, an eerie raag that we use a lot for the Kauravas. There's a lot of dissonance and off-notes.

It's clear that a lot of discipline goes into the apparent freedom of improvisational music. Why is the discipline of training in classical Indian music so important to what we hear in *Mahabharata*?

HL: Even after our eight-hour rehearsals in the studio, [Zaheer-]Abbas [Janmohamed], the tabla player, and I would go home and practise for two or three hours more. We'd say, 'Look, we didn't actually get to play as much as we wanted to.' We had so much music in our heads that we had to just release it.

The reason is that through discipline comes freedom. Once you train your voice to express your emotions, then you have the freedom to do that whenever you want. It almost has to become second nature, so that when you're onstage surrounded by all these other musicians, you have the freedom to just play and express.

Was part of you playing after hours with Abbas about developing a shared understanding?

HL: Yeah, and also because we had never worked together before. There are lots of different styles of classical music. We call it gharana, which is essentially a particular school of music teaching. It's all classical music, but the finer expressions are different.

A CONVERSATION
ON THE *BHAGAVAD GITA*

*Sharada K Eswar is a playwright, storyteller, and educator based in Brampton,
Canada, who translated and adapted the text of the* Bhagavad Gita. *She is also the*
Khana and Kahani *storyteller and has been an artistic associate on* Mahabharata
throughout its development.

**What was your role in creating the *Bhagavad Gita* operatic aria sung
during *Dharma*?**

Sharada K Eswar: As the artistic associate on this project, my role was to
make sure that factually things were in place and that the core story was
intact. The *Bhagavad Gita*, or the Celestial Song, is a very important part of
the *Mahabharata*. It takes place on Day 1 of the battle, and it is a discourse
between Arjuna and Krishna. Until then, Krishna has taken a back seat in
the story. It is only here in act 7 of the *Mahabharata* that he plays a key role.

When Vyasa wrote the entire epic, it was not considered a religious
text. It's just the *Bhagavad Gita* that has become sacred. It encompasses the
key principles of what Hinduism is. When I say Hinduism, I mean a Hindu
philosophy of life.

I was tasked with curating the *Bhagavad Gita* into a sixteen-minute
libretto. What I essentially did was to take the key points that the *Gita*
touches upon and that are relevant to the show itself.

One of the things the *Gita* talks about is detachment, which is not
about renouncing materialism or going away to the Himalayas and medi-
tating. It is about, 'How does one be part of a society and yet be apart
from it?' The *Gita* says that happiness is not defined by who you are or
how you are viewed by others. Happiness is contained within you. We
look for happiness everywhere but within ourselves.

**You have a background as a classically trained musician. How were
you musically engaged with curating the *Gita*?**

SKE: When we learn these shlokas from the *Gita*, or hymns as they're
sometimes called, there's a certain rhythm, like a chant. The very first

shloka I learned from my grandmother. So there is always musicality to it – that is how I was hearing it. I've heard Meher sing it so many times in the show, but I hear it in my head as a child sitting in the audience.

I'm trained in Carnatic South Indian classical music. I know Suba [Sankaran] has her grounding in South Indian classical music as well. So to hear those melodies was absolutely delightful. I think it's very different from the arias one would normally hear.

Especially toward the end, the notes that she's singing – that's the foundation of Carnatic music, the seven notes, the seven swaras. They're like scales. It's like do-re-mis, those are the building blocks. Any South Asian – you go for dance classes, you go for music lessons – they would've all recognized that.

Meher (the performer of the aria) mentioned that she consulted with you every day while she was preparing the aria. What did you discuss?

SKE: Basically, we were working on pronunciation. It was interesting for me because I take these verses for granted. There are layers and layers to each word. So you have to look beyond what that word literally means to know what it means at an emotional level, a spiritual level, a metaphysical level.

Also, it was exciting to go back to a language that is very different from any of the European languages. The Sanskrit language has no clear opposites. As we discuss in the *Khana* part of the production, dharma and adharma are not the same thing as right versus wrong. They're two sides of the same coin.

اللّٰه

Suba Sankaran is a composer and musician based in Toronto, Canada. Suba Sankaran and John Gzowski were the co-composers of the Bhagavad Gita *opera.*

What was the brief that you received from Ravi and Miriam to create this aria?

Suba Sankaran: They gave us many, many sheets of paper that had the verses of the *Bhagavad Gita*, both in Sanskrit written phonetically and the English translation beside it. John [Gzowski] and I thought, 'Let's choose the ones that still give a good arc for the story so that we're not missing some crucial element.' We skipped a few, and then there's a big gap toward the end.

To set it to music, we divided up the verses and settled on a key. We decided we were going to use different constructs that happen in both South and North Indian classical music.

The opening, the first four verses, is free from the rigours of time. It's meant to be floating and sort of elastic, so you're not going to hear any rhythm in that part.

Ravi had said he really liked certain Baroque operas, and I have a few of my own favourites, like *Dido and Aeneas*. In the orchestration, we added in some harpsichord, but still with all these Sanskrit lyrics.

We had a debate about language. Eventually, they went with the surtitles in English and sung in Sanskrit, which I think was a great move. It loses something of its ancient nature in English translation if you were to sing it, but to have it in the surtitles gives this deeper meaning, especially for a Western audience.

Then we went through and explored different ragas. Sometimes we were within the rules of the raga, and sometimes we were not; we had the freedom to go either way.

Close to the end, there's a big climax, and we have Meher singing in sound syllables that are relatively meaningless. She's riffing on that and does the same thing three times. It takes a left turn because she does this amazing climax, and then we get some text spoken by Arjuna, and then it goes back full circle, where the opera singer goes into a three-tone chant. These were all ideas that we had in order to stay true to the culture it's coming from, but still working in a way where harmony, which doesn't exist in Indian music, can play a huge role.

مله

Meher Pavri is an actor and singer based in London, Canada, who performs the Voice of Krishna.

How well did you know the *Bhagavad Gita* before this production?

Meher Pavri: If you walk into any yoga studio, they have a copy of it there. But my first encounter with the text was through this aria. And it blew my mind, even just singing in Sanskrit. It's so close to what I pray in, a language called Avestan. It's not a spoken language anymore, but it has similar words and sounds.

It was moving because it reminded me of my dad, who is a Zoroastrian priest. He would be praying and chanting at home all the time, and I would hear him in the background. It sounded similar to what I'm singing now. A lot of people ask me, 'How long did it take you to learn this Sanskrit?' But there was already something so natural about this for me.

Was learning the *Gita* different than other operatic texts?

MP: I've never sung some of these sounds before. I've sung in about ten different languages for opera purposes, but never in Sanskrit. To be able to sing the *Gita* in its original text is so special. Especially for those who have this religious affiliation with it.

Do you believe an operatic rendering is a good fit for the *Gita* text?

MP: Totally. I remember thinking, 'This is such an important part of *Mahabharata*. How are they going to do it?' To keep the grandeur of the emotion, and to portray something so epic, they thought of opera.

Getting to collaborate with Suba and John was a dream, because they literally had my voice in mind when they composed it. And with all of us being in the room together, they would ask me things like, 'How does that feel for you?' I can't go back and have a conversation with Mozart about an aria. I got to pick their brains about why they made musical choices.

How do you understand this character? Who is this singer?

MP: I am Krishna. There's only one verse where I sing as Arjuna; I'm essentially a version of Krishna the whole show. Right before I come on, the Storyteller says, 'Krishna unravels the mysteries of the universe.'

After the intermission, I'm still a version of Krishna. I'm watching everything unravel. And I am adding sounds, I'm humming throughout the whole second half of the show.

And then at the end, the last thing that I say in English is, 'Nothing and no one lasts,' which is another composition from Suba and John. The whole song didn't make it into the show, but we added that one verse. And it just encompasses everything.

During the performance, you have tremendous focus and energy. How did you work on characterization?

MP: I got musical notes from Suba and John all the time. And I would tweak it every day with Sharada. She would have a list of Sanskrit words for me to fix. And I worked with Ravi on the direction and the movement of the staging.

And then I had walking classes with Brandy, the choreographer. It was a revelation to work on slow-motion walking. A lot of mornings, as a group, the other actors and I would do slow-motion movement. We worked on getting slower, and slower, and slower. I have to practise it every day – to also be able to sustain long notes on one foot sometimes is a challenge. But I think it's important because it transports everyone into a different state.

KEY TERMS AND CONCEPTS

By Lawrence Switzky with Sharada K Eswar

(Note: **Karma** and **dharma** are discussed at length in the interview with Devdutt Pattanaik and throughout the other interviews.)

RITUALS AND PERFORMANCES

Why Not Theatre's *Mahabharata* begins with **pranam**, salutations by the actors, who are seeking blessings for their performance. By doing pranam, you literally bow and greet someone, but you also symbolically show your reverence for another who has walked so many miles before you. That's why the feet are so important in pranam – you are acknowledging metaphorically how far they have travelled. In this production, the actors seek blessings from Mother Earth specifically. Their pranam recognizes that they are performing on the earth and asks forgiveness for any sins they might commit while doing so.

Actors also perform **mudras** during the performance. Mudras are hand gestures that are mostly used in dance. They symbolize gods or characters. Vishnu is often portrayed with a disc in one hand and a conch in the other; when you see an actor twirling their forefinger, they're making the mudra for Vishnu's disc.

Audiences will also encounter musical cues from the band and the actors. The **tihai**, the final three notes in Indian classical music, indicate the end of a song; in this production, they cue the Storyteller to begin speaking. In *Dharma*, actors clap a **talam**, a rhythmic beat, and voice **solkattu**, a form of vocal percussion that can sound like 'taku, taku' and 'ta, ta' (*solkattu* is two words joined together: *sol* is a syllable, and *kattu* is a bundle – a bundle of syllables).

In *Karma*, Kunti and Madri use a **mantra** to become pregnant with the Pandava children. A mantra can be a word or a sound, but often it's a chanted hymn that gives you magical powers. Kunti has learned this mantra from a travelling sage who visited her father's court, and who gave her the power to invoke the gods because he was so pleased with her attentiveness. The sage, in turn, acquired the mantra through years of prayer and meditation.

A **swayamvara** is a series of festive contests in which a woman has agency to choose her own husband. The woman gets to invite who competes for her as well as specific tests of their worthiness, and these can be both battles of wits and battles of strength. In this *Mahabharata*, we witness both Amba's and Draupadi's swayamvaras, specifically in the form of archery competitions; these challenges are segments in a larger event.

CLASSES AND SPECIES

The characters in *Mahabharata* belong to social classes that were established long before these stories were first told. There are four classes, based on the professions. The Pandavas and the Kauravas are **kshatriyas**, members of the warrior class. Their job is to defend their society, city, and nation. The **brahmins** are educators. Commerce, trade, and agriculture are in the hands of the **vaishyas**. And the job of the **shudras** is to ensure that the infrastructure of the city is in top condition. We often see conflicts or misunderstandings between the classes in *Mahabharata*. Drona is a brahmin. Ekalavya belongs to the shudras. At the time *Mahabharata* was written, these classes locked horns to determine who was superior. The kshatriyas claimed they were superior because of their job – they were so brave, they were so courageous. And the brahmins said, we are educators, we hold power, we are superior. During this jockeying for position among the brahmins and the kshatriyas, the vaishyas and the shudras became the lower classes, and that unfortunately continues to this day.

We also witness conflicts between the human and the nonhuman worlds. The **nagas** are a race of snakes who rule the netherworld and are vested with special powers, particularly over the weather. The **yakshas**, on the other hand, are forest spirits and demigods. They can be affiliated with any of the natural elements. The yaksha who tests Yudhishthira in this *Mahabharata* is a water spirit.

STORIES WITHIN THE STORY

Audiences who attend the **khana** (meal) and hear a **kahani** (story) will encounter the **akshayapatra**, a never-ending pot of food that was given to Draupadi while in exile and that continues to produce food each day until she has finished eating. It appears in a story in *Mahabharata* in which Krishna, in a mischievous mood, plays a prank on the Pandavas and nearly gets them in trouble with a visiting sage who demands food. In this performance, the akshayapatra refers metaphorically to any pot or kitchen that keeps on giving.

In *Dharma*, the **Chakravyuha** occurs at a climactic moment in the battle at Kurukshetra. It's a battle formation made of two Sanskrit words: *chakra* (wheel) and *vyuha* (maze). From an aerial view, the perspective of the gods, it looks like a wheel. It's also sometimes called the Padmavyuha, where *padma* is a lotus and *vyuha* (again) is a maze. From above, the formation resembles a tightly closed lotus flower. To breach it, you need to know a mantra, and that mantra opens one of the petals, which is made up of soldiers: foot soldiers, soldiers on horses, elephants, chariots. The commander is positioned in the centre of the Chakravyuha. But you have to penetrate layers and layers of soldiers to find him. There are only a few people in the world who know how to form this maze, and who know the mantras to get in and out. Drona, who sets the formation, is one. Krishna is another because he knows everything. Abhimanyu, Arjuna's son, also knows because he heard his parents discussing this battle formation when he was still in the womb and heard the mantra that is required to get in. But just as Arjuna was about to describe how to get out, he noticed his wife was falling asleep, and he didn't want to wake her. So Abhimanyu knows how to get in but not how to leave once he's inside. At a philosophical level, this story is about how we treat our children. We give them only half the information they need to know, we don't respect them, and then they get into trouble. In this case, it's fatal.

We hear a number of references to **thirty-six years** in *Dharma*. After the death of Duryodhana, Gandhari curses Krishna that he and his family will perish in thirty-six years. After the events at Kurukshetra, we hear that Yudhishthira will be the dharma king for thirty-six years. In both cases, that's how long is left in the current age, or **yuga**. There are four cyclical epochs in Hindu cosmology. One is the Satya Yuga, the first and best or 'golden' age, then the Treta Yuga, and then the Dvapara Yuga, and then the Kali Yuga. They repeat, and they last hundreds of thousands of years: this is time not as we know it on Earth, but in a cosmic or divine sense. *Mahabharata* takes place at the end of the third epoch, the Dvapara Yuga, and thirty-six years remain in that epoch. The age that begins at the conclusion of that age, the Kali Yuga, is the yuga we're currently in. Dharma has the upper hand in the Satya Yuga, and then it starts to fall and adharma (actions that contribute to disorder and disharmony) begins to rise in the subsequent ages. In our yuga, adharma is at its peak.

Dharma concludes with a discussion about **jaya.** Jaya is a special kind of victory: not over external forces, as in battle (the word for that is *vijaya*), but over oneself. At the end of *Mahabharata*, Yudhishthira achieves jaya. He learns that his brothers are in hell and that Duryodhana is enjoying life in heaven – even though there is no hell or heaven in Hinduism. He's holding on to a lot of anger. But he lets go of his anger, and his happiness, and everything else, and through that he attains jaya. That's the victory *Mahabharata* teaches us to aim for. This *Mahabharata* ends with the chant 'Om, Shanti, Shanti, Shanti,' which means peace. That's how rituals that involve fire end. It calms the fire down: not the fire outside, but the fire within you. When you achieve that stillness and that calm, you can find true jaya.

ACKNOWLEDGEMENTS

This *Mahabharata* has been tended to and nourished by a community that spans the world. This is an attempt to acknowledge those people who have surrounded, supported, and inspired us over the past eight years.

One of the greatest respites during our journey of adapting this text has been spending time with past tellers of the epic. For thousands of years before the story was written down, it was passed from generation to generation orally, and so there are as many *Mahabharatas* as there are storytellers. Assembling this version has been an enormous task of compilation. In compiling this *Mahabharata*, we turned to many sutra-dharas, which translates from Sanskrit as 'the person who weaves the threads.' We want to express gratitude to a few key storytellers who have held up lanterns to help us see in the sometimes dark forest. Our love and respect to Sharada K Eswar, Devdutt Pattanaik, Rustom Bharucha, Peter Brook and Jean-Claude Carrière, Rabindranath Tagore, B. R. Chopra, Amar Chitra Katha, and our deepest thanks to Carole Satyamurti, whose poetry and imagination have anchored our journey.

Beyond the circle of sutradharas, our eternal thanks to all those who helped us breathe this text to life onstage, and now into a book. To the Why Not Theatre team, past and present, who believed in this project and, like Krishna, pulled off a miracle and lifted this mountain of a show on one finger.

To the cast, designers, and stage management team of the premiere production, thank you for your artistry, energy, and questions. The patience and love with which you received constant edits made this script possible.

To all the artists, designers, stage managers, and producers who contributed to the development workshops of the show over eight years, thank you for helping us tend to the forest of stories and carve multiple paths through it.

To the teams at the Shaw Festival (to TC, who initially approached us with this idea to collaborate) and the Barbican Centre, whose theatres housed our premieres and allowed us to meet our first audiences.

To Karen, Larry, Alana, and Crystal for helping to take this ephemeral art of theatre and transform it into something that we can hold.

To our families: Sturla, Maria, Ernest, Josh, Julia, Vish, Maya, Sarena, Rohan, and Simran, thank you for your love and support, and for listening to us talk about this story for what feels like 4,000 years.

And finally, to the ancestors: parents, grandparents, aunties, and uncles who have passed down this story for generations, thank you for keeping it alive so that we may inherit it.

ॐ

Why Not Theatre acknowledges that the world premiere of *Mahabharata* would not be possible without the support of the Canada Council for the Arts, the National Arts Centre's National Creation Fund, the Government of Ontario, the Slaight Family Foundation, Deb Barrett and Jim Leech, the Kingfisher Foundation, the Lindy Green Family Foundation, and the Wuchien Michael Than Foundation.

ॐ

Photographs (pp. 17–24) are used with permission of the photographer David Cooper. The top photograph on p. 18 is used with permission of the photographer Michael Cooper. Images feature the cast of Why Not Theatre's *Mahabharata* (Shaw Festival, 2023).

ABOUT THE AUTHORS

Ravi Jain and Miriam Fernandes, Co-Writers and Adapters

Ravi and Miriam are co-artistic directors of the internationally renowned Why Not Theatre. Both graduates of the Lecoq School in Paris, they are well known as devisor/collaborators who make work from the ground up. They are theatre makers, switching hats from acting to writing to directing. Together they collaborated on the theatre production and film of *What You Won't Do For Love*, starring David Suzuki and Tara Cullis, and *Mahabharata*. Both scripts are published by Coach House Books.

Ravi Jain's work has been seen on stages both big and small around the world. Published plays include *A Brimful of Asha*, *What You Won't Do For Love*, and *Mahabharata*. Ravi often adapts classical texts, including the celebrated English/ASL production of *Prince Hamlet* (with Dawn Jani Birley), and *R + J*, an adaptation of *Romeo and Juliet* for sighted, blind, and low-vision audiences at the Stratford Festival (with Alex Bulmer and Christine Horne).

Miriam Fernandes is a Toronto-based artist who has worked as an actor, director, and theatre-maker across Canada, USA, Norway, France, and Australia. Her adaptation of Gogol's *The Nose* (*Nesen*) premiered at the MiniMidiMaxi Festival in Norway and continued on to tour the country. She is currently developing a new adaptation of Ibsen's *Enemy of the People*.

Sharada K Eswar, Text Adaptation and Translation, *Bhagavad Gita*

Sharada is a South Asian–Canadian playwright, storyteller, and theatre maker, committed to telling stories about people of colour. Sharada has garnered artistic credits at the National Arts Centre (Playwright in Residence, 2017), Theatre Direct, Jumblies Theatre, Tamasha Arts, Why Not Theatre, and Soulpepper Theatre, to name a few. Recent stage work includes *The Draupadi Project, Butter Chicken,* and *The Death of Abhimanyu.* Sharada has been the recipient of several awards, including the prestigious JAYU award for an established artist and the OAAG Award for the best community arts project. A published author, her new book, *When the Banyan Sways,* will be published in 2024 by Running the Goat Books and Broadsides. She is currently the Artistic Director of Jumblies Theatre.

Vedavyasa, Original Author, *Mahabharata*

Vyasena grathitam Purana muninaa *Mahabharatham* … Krishna Dvaipayana, better known as Vedavyasa, is traditionally regarded as the author of the epic *Mahabharata.* Born to Satyavati and the sage Parashara, Vyasa is also regarded as a partial incarnation of Vishnu and the compiler of the mantras of the Vedas (the oldest layer of Sanskrit literature) as well as the author of the eighteen Puranas and the Brahma Sutras. He is one of the eight Chiranjeevis (immortals who are to remain on Earth until the end of the current epoch).

Typeset in Albertina, Times New Roman, and Fold–No. 21.

Printed at the Coach House on bpNichol Lane in Toronto, Ontario, Rolland Opaque Natural paper, which was manufactured in Saint-Jérôme, Quebec. This book was printed with vegetable-based ink on a 1973 Heidelberg KORD offset litho press. Its pages were folded on a Baumfolder, gathered by hand, bound on a Sulby Auto-Minabinda, and trimmed on a Polar single-knife cutter.

Coach House is on the traditional territory of many nations including the Mississaugas of the Credit, the Anishnabeg, the Chippewa, the Haudenosaunee, and the Wendat peoples, and is now home to many diverse First Nations, Inuit, and Métis peoples. We acknowledge that Toronto is covered by Treaty 13 with the Mississaugas of the Credit. We are grateful to live and work on this land.

Compiled by Karen Fricker and Lawrence Switzky
Cover design by Humble Raja: Bhavesh & Reena Mistry
Interior design by Crystal Sikma
Author photo by David Cooper

Coach House Books
80 bpNichol Lane
Toronto ON M5S 3J4
Canada

416 979 2217
800 367 6360

mail@chbooks.com
www.chbooks.com